D0562531

WHY DO
CATHOLICS...?

WHY DO CATHOLICS...?

Teens Respond
to Questions
about The Faith

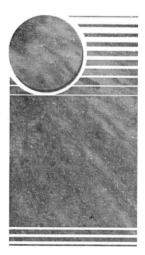

Michael J. Daley,
editor

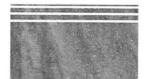

The publishing team included Laurie Delgatto and Maura Thompson Hagarty, development editors; Lorraine Kilmartin, reviewer; prepress and manufacturing coordinated by the production departments of Saint Mary's Press.

Copyright © 2007 by Saint Mary's Press, Christian Brothers Publications, 702 Terrace Heights, Winona, MN 55987-1318, www.smp .org. All rights reserved. No part of this book may be reproduced by any means without the written permission of the publisher.

Sabrina Minonne, cover image

Printed in the United States of America

3445

ISBN 978-0-88489-915-0

Library of Congress Cataloging-in-Publication Data

Why do Catholics-- ? : teens respond to questions about the faith / Michael J. Daley, editor.
    p. cm.
ISBN 978-0-88489-915-0 (pbk.)
    1. Catholic teenagers—Religious life—Miscellanea. 2. Catholic Church—Doctrines—Miscellanea. I. Daley, Michael J., 1968-

BX2355.W49 2007
282—dc22
                                                        2007003243

Dedication

I dedicate this book to all my students—past, present, and future.

Author Acknowledgments

I wish to extend my heartfelt thanks to the contributors and those who invited the contributors to participate. Without you this book would not have been possible. Also, I would like to thank Laurie Delgatto and Maura Hagarty of Saint Mary's Press, who entrusted me with this project and helped bring it to completion. Finally, thanks to my family—June, Cara, Brendan, and Nora—who gave me the time and encouragement to complete this project.

Contents

Chapter 2: Teens Share Their Understanding of Jesus

Chapter 3: Teens Share Their Understanding of the Scriptures

Chapter 4: Teens Share Their Understanding of the Mass (Liturgy) and the Sacraments

Chapter 5: Teens Share Their Understanding of Prayer and Spirituality

Chapter 6: Teens Share Their Understanding of Mary and the Saints

Chapter 7: Teens Share Their Understanding of Teenage Life Issues

Introduction

It All Begins
with a Question

In light of perennial natural disasters, a question is raised: If God is all powerful and all loving, why would God allow such seemingly innocent suffering? For several years now, many have asked if the present form of priestly ministry can be changed and opened to married men, even women. Recent presidential elections have brought up the confusing question of whether Catholics should base their votes on a single issue or consider a spectrum of life issues. The war, new technologies in medicine, continued environmental degradation, ever-present issues of sexuality. . . . It can all be overwhelming.

As a teacher, I experience firsthand the struggles young people have with integrating their understanding of faith and Tradition with all that happens around them. You'd think that just as a coping mechanism, teenagers would stop asking questions. Nope. Young people continue to question, wanting all the more to see a connection with what they believe and what is going on in the real world.

When I was asked by Saint Mary's Press to consider writing a book for young people on questions and answers of faith, I was both intrigued and excited about the idea. But the more I considered it, the more I found myself asking, "If I were a young person, would I want to hear answers about questions of faith from yet another adult?" Then it struck me—why not let young people ask and answer their own questions of faith? So that is exactly what I did. Rather than offer my own responses to such questions, I extended an invitation to young people to serve as the authors of this book.

This book offers personal answers written by teens to the many questions, wonderings, and challenges they and many of their peers face regarding the practices and beliefs of the Catholic Church. In these pages, teenage authors share their own understanding of the Catholic Tradition, and their personal experiences (and challenges) of integrating faith with the real world.

Though this book does not answer every question you have about Catholicism, it will offer you some clear guidance and direction as you continue to navigate through the joys and challenges we all face as Catholic Christians.

Keep questioning, keep developing, and keep expanding your faith.

Mike Daley

Teens Share Their Understanding **of Catholic Beliefs and Practices**

How Does Catholicism Differ from Other Christian Traditions?

Mike Wren
Brophy College Preparatory, Phoenix, Arizona

The authority of the Catholic Church was established at the moment Jesus said, "You are Peter, and on this rock I will build my church" (Matthew 16:18). Other churches—Episcopal, Methodist, Lutheran, Baptist, Quaker, Pentecostal, and so on—were established by men who chose to separate themselves from full communion with the Catholic Church.

All Christian traditions share the common belief that salvation comes only through Christ. However, there are many areas in which other Christian traditions and Catholicism differ.

All Christians believe that God's complete revelation is expressed in Jesus Christ. All Christians believe that the Bible is a primary way of communicating God's revelation, but Catholics believe that God's revelation is also communicated through sacred Tradition.

All Christians believe the Bible is true and without error when it teaches the things God wishes to reveal to us for the sake of our salvation. Some Christians also believe the Bible is without error in every aspect, including references to scientific and historical facts. But Catholics, along with other Christians, are cautious about making this claim. The Catholic Church teaches that in order to interpret the Bible correctly, we must understand what the human authors intended to communicate at the time of their writings.

In the area of morality, the Catholic Church believes in absolute, objective truth, meaning there is good and evil. The Catholic Church proclaims the person of Jesus and promotes a culture of life.

Another way the Catholic Church is set apart from some other denominations is through the celebration of the seven sacraments. Some Christian traditions question whether the sacraments are a necessary part of Church life. But Catholics believe that Jesus gave the sacraments, his very presence, to the Church to help his people obtain God's sanctifying grace and truly experience union with Christ. Some Protestant traditions also do not believe in the centrality of the Eucharist, and some do not celebrate the Eucharist or do so only occasionally.

Catholics also believe in the role of the Pope as the head of the Church. Many Protestant traditions do not believe in any kind of centralized leadership.

Unlike some denominations, the Catholic Church also believes in the communion of saints. Just as our friends on earth care about us and pray for us, the saints also intercede for us with God. They are, in a way, a sort of lifeline. We pray through them and with them and ask them to pray for us. The lives of the saints inspire us to be better members of the Body of Christ.

What Are the Marks of the Church?

Ryan D'sa
Saint Ignatius High School, Cleveland, Ohio

There are actually four specific marks that distinguish the Catholic Christian Church: *one, holy, catholic,* and *apostolic.* As Catholics we proclaim these marks every Sunday when we recite the Nicene Creed. The creed is one of the most powerful prayers of our faith, and it reminds us of the beliefs of all Catholics. However, it is important to note that the Nicene Creed belongs to all Christians, not just Catholics. Other Christians understand or stress different marks of the Church than Catholics do.

The first mark of the Church is *one*. This means that the Church is one in Christ, faith, and prayer. The Church being one is a sign of unity. This gift comes from the Spirit and helps us to live like Jesus. The Church is one in faith, worship, government, and charity. One in faith means that we believe in the same things. One in worship means that we share in the same Eucharist. We are one in government through our Church leaders. We are one in charity because we give of our time, talent, and treasure to those in need, both inside and outside our faith community.

The second mark of the Church is *holy*. The Church is holy because Christ founded her and the Holy Spirit guides her. The Catholic Church is holy through the seven sacraments. Through the sacraments, our relationship with God is strengthened, and we grow in our faith.

The third mark of the Church is *catholic*. The word *catholic* means "universal" or "worldwide." The Church is catholic because it preaches the Good News to all people. It teaches the message of Christ and offers all that is needed for salvation. The Church is called catholic because it adapts to all ages and generations. All the people of the Church help strengthen this mark when they preach the word of God and when they do good deeds for others.

The last mark of the Church is *apostolic*. This means that the Church is rooted in the beliefs of the Apostles and continues their mission. The Church is apostolic through its whole governance hierarchy and the body of believers. We are all called to be apostolic and help the Church follow in the footsteps of the Apostles.

As much as the Church is one, holy, catholic, and apostolic, it is also sometimes marked by division, sin, sectarianism, and confusion.

The marks, then, have been achieved but can also be more fully realized.

Why Does the Catholic Church Have a Pope? Is He Infallible?

Megan M. Tuohy
Brebeuf Jesuit Preparatory School, Indianapolis, Indiana

The Pope is the leader of the Catholic Church. He is Saint Peter's successor. This is demonstrated in the Scriptures when Jesus changes Simon's name to Peter and says, "You are Peter, and on this rock I will build my church" (Matthew 16:18). In the Gospel of John, the resurrected Jesus instructs Peter, "Tend my sheep" (21:17). From this scriptural testimony evolved the ministry of the bishop of Rome to shepherd the Church.

The succession of the papacy offers a faithful line to Jesus and his teachings for members of the Catholic Church. Today—as seen especially through the ministry of the last Pope, Pope John Paul II, and now Pope Benedict XVI—the Pope serves as a visible symbol of Church unity.

An often disputed and misunderstood teaching associated with the Pope is that of infallibility. Infallibility is a great gift God has given the Church; it means that we can rely on the Church's teachings as being true. The Pope is "empowered with the infallibility that Christ conferred on his Church." (*Encyclopedia of Catholicism*, page 664). The ability to speak infallibly is the Pope's highest authority, but not all popes choose to exercise such authority.

However, only the Church can define teachings in the areas of faith and moral issues as infallible or free from error. To be clear, not every statement of every pope is an infallible statement. The Pope must declare that he is speaking infallibly in order for his words to be documented as free from error.

There are other conditions to the Pope's authority to speak infallibly, including (1) that others can speak infallibly along with the Pope (usually bishops in a Church council), (2) that his speaking as infallible is not his alone but represents the beliefs of all Christians, (3) that the matters of which he speaks must be linked to revelation, and (4) that the Pope is not speaking from his own capacity but from a "divine assistance" (*Encyclopedia of Catholicism*, page 664).

Why Are There So Many Christian Denominations?

Alex Craven
Saint Xavier High School, Cincinnati, Ohio

A great philosopher once said: "There was nothing funny about what Christ said; what was funny really is that Christ said all these really good things about 'love thy neighbor' and everything, and then for the next 2,000 years, people are killing each other, and torturing each other because they can't quite decide how he said it" (*Monty Python's Flying Circus: Live at Aspen*, 1998).

Divisions in the Church go back to the first century. In his First Letter to the Corinthians, the Apostle Paul lamented that strife and divisions had resulted in some saying, "'I belong to Paul,' and another, 'I belong to Apollos'" (1 Corinthians 3:4). A separation occurred within the Church in 1054 when the Greek-speaking Church of the East separated from the Latin-based Church in the West over a number of political and cultural differences, along with some relatively minor doctrinal disputes. The Church in the East became known as the Eastern Orthodox Church, and the Church in the West was called the Roman Catholic Church. These main divisions continue today.

Later, reformers among the Roman Catholics felt a need for spiritual renewal and correction within the Church. They especially protested the addition of nonbiblical tradition to the Bible as essential to the faith and practice of Christianity. These protesting reformers eventually brought about a second major separation. From the Protestant Reformation came the Lutheran, Calvinist, Baptist, and other denominations. There were then splits from the splits, and faith communities like Puritans and Calvinists formed. Now there are countless different Christian communities all over the world.

Though there are differences between denominations, most of the basic doctrines agreed on by the early Catholic Church are still accepted by all. For example, Roman Catholics, Eastern Orthodox religions, most Protestants, and most Evangelical religions believe in the Trinity and in the divinity of Christ, and all Christian denominations agree that Jesus Christ died to atone for the sins of the world and was raised from the grave to break the power of Satan and death.

It is important not to become so preoccupied with the minor differences between the denominations that we overlook their broad areas of agreement. Much has been done to bring the churches closer together, but much more needs to take place.

What Was **Vatican II?**

Anthony DeWees
Father Lopez High School, Daytona Beach, Florida

Vatican II, also known as the Second Vatican Council, was an ecumenical council—a gathering of all the world's bishops. It took place over forty years ago and seems like ancient history to most young people. However, to our grandparents (and maybe even some of our parents), it was one of the most important religious occurrences of their lives. Vatican II has had a major effect on the lives of many Catholics.

The council was started by Pope John XXIII on October 11, 1962, and was concluded by Pope Paul VI on December 8, 1965. During the council, close to three thousand bishops discussed major reforms of the Catholic Church. The four sessions were held at Saint Peter's

Basilica in Rome. As a result of Vatican II, many changes were made to the Catholic faith.

The first, and perhaps most tangible, effect of the council was the transforming changes made to the liturgy. Prior to Vatican II, Mass was prayed in Latin, which many people did not understand. The priest even stood with his back to the gathered assembly. As a result, the congregation did not actively participate much in the liturgy.

Now the Mass is said in the vernacular, or local, language. Now people understand more fully what is happening at Mass. As an assembly, we are encouraged to actively participate in the liturgy, and the priest now faces the congregation. All these changes are the result of Vatican II.

The council also encouraged and gave Catholics the tools to read the Bible. Vatican II redefined the Church's relationship with Judaism and spoke of the importance of dialogue with other world religions. It also sought to overcome deep division among the various Christian traditions.

The council called for greater collegiality among the bishops and the Pope. The council reaffirmed the Pope's role as the sole successor of Peter and upheld the importance of Mary.

Finally, especially as it concerns young Catholics, Vatican II stressed and called for the active involvement of the laity, the people in the pews.

Does (Has) the Church Ever Change(d)?

Erin McKenna
Christian Brothers High School, Sacramento, California

The Church has to be willing to adapt because the world changes and each generation is different from the one before it. Because the Church is the community charged with continuing Jesus's mission on earth, it has to be able to respond to new and different questions and circumstances.

It is important to emphasize that God's revelation does not change. What evolves is the Church's understanding of God's word. Another way of saying this is that our fundamental beliefs don't change, but sometimes the way we understand and explain our beliefs and the way we apply them to what is happening in the world changes. For example, there was a time when the Church did not recognize that slavery was unjust, but now it does.

Our practices can change too. Some of the most noticeable during the last half century are changes in our liturgical practices. The Second Vatican Council (1962–1965) ushered in quite a few, including a change in the language used at Mass. Before Vatican II, the Mass was prayed in Latin. Since the council, Catholics around the world have celebrated Mass using the vernacular, their common, everyday language.

So some things about the Church change, but its most important aspects stay the same.

Can Jews, Muslims, and Other Non-Christians **Be Saved?**

Dylan Perry
Christian Brothers High School, Memphis, Tennessee

Of course those who are not Catholic can be saved. The Catholic Church would not be so presumptuous as to assume that it holds the corner market on salvation. Catholics do not claim that those who do not believe in Jesus are going to hell. What the Church does teach is that Jesus is the fullest, clearest, and most complete way of salvation. It also admits and allows for Jesus's presence to be found and communicated beyond the visible bonds of the Church.

To take a rather extreme example, say that there is a remote tribe in the mountains of South America. The members of the tribe have never had the opportunity to learn about Jesus Christ or to be baptized into Christianity. Catholics believe that it would hardly be fair to condemn the most morally upstanding of these people to an eternity of torment simply because they do not have access to the Bible or to missionaries to teach them the Gospel. Doing so would essentially be damning a person for being born in the wrong place, to the wrong group, at the wrong time.

To take this example a little further, say that a man from this village found out about Jesus but saw no reason to change his beliefs. It would not be fair to say that because he didn't convert to Christianity, he should go to hell. If his religious tradition works for him and teaches the same core values as Christianity, it doesn't matter if he calls his God Jesus, Vishnu, Yahweh, or Allah.

I have a Hindu friend who is a good person and follows his religion. I also have a friend who is a very devout Muslim. It would be very hard for me to believe that God would persecute them simply because they believe or worship in a different way.

How Does Someone Join the Catholic Church?

Heather DeLucenay
Marian High School, Mishawaka, Indiana

People who are interested in joining the Catholic Church typically participate in a program called the *Rite of Christian Initiation of Adults,* or RCIA for short.

There are four stages in the RCIA program. The first stage is known as the period of inquiry. This is a time where program participants (known as inquirers) explore the Catholic faith and share their own faith experiences with others who are not Catholics as well as with those who make up the RCIA leadership team. This period is intended to help the inquirers decide if they really want to join the Catholic Church.

If an inquirer decides to continue the process, he or she then enters into a period called the *catechumenate* and become what is known as a *catechumen* (one who is preparing for full initiation into the Church) or a *candidate* (one who is preparing for the sacraments of Holy Communion and Confirmation).

During this time, the catechumens and candidates, with the support and assistance of sponsors, examine the Catholic faith more deeply. Each Sunday the catechumens and candidates are invited to participate in the liturgy of the word and are dismissed after the proclamation of the Gospel to examine more fully God's word and its application to their lives. This is all done to better prepare the catechumens and candidates to become fully initiated members of the community.

The third period of the process, known as the period of *illumination,* coincides with the forty days of Lent. During this time, there is a process of taking a deeper look into the catechumens' and candidates' lives. It is often considered the most intense part of the RCIA process.

On Holy Saturday (the night before Easter) during the Vigil Mass, the catechumens are baptized, receive first Communion, and are confirmed. Candidates (who have already been baptized in another Christian faith) receive first Communion and are confirmed. At this time, they are finally considered fully initiated members of the Catholic community.

Mystagogia is the final stage of the RCIA process, but it is in turn the beginning of a pilgrimage of lifelong, continuous conversion in full communion with the Roman Catholic community of Christians.

Where Does the Church Stand in the Debate Between Evolution and Creationism?

Eric Prister

Marian High School, Mishawaka, Indiana

Since the publication of Charles Darwin's *The Origin of Species* in 1859, the theory of evolution has been a fierce debate in religious circles. The theory of creationism (based on a literal reading of the Book of Genesis) had always been the accepted theory, and many were slow (and some still haven't) to accept Darwin's revolutionary idea. Both theories have countless supporters with legitimate arguments and concerns.

The theory of evolution claims that life on earth was originally made up of only one-celled organisms. These organisms evolved over billions of years into the many species known today. Humans, of course, are no exception. Many people are against this theory because humans are believed to be God's chosen people, created in God's image.

The theory of creationism states that God created everything on earth as it says in Genesis, chapters 1 and 2 (there are two Creation stories). The theory of evolution does not seem to agree with the story of Creation found in the Book of Genesis when the Creation story is taken literally. Without the literal interpretations, Catholics can believe, for example, that the animals created could have evolved into humans during that same "day." Of course, "one day" here would not mean one twenty-four-hour period of time. One day could equal billions of years. For Catholics, the Creation story in Genesis is understood as a story expressing religious truth, not scientific fact.

In an address to the Pontifical Academy of Sciences (October 3, 1981), Pope John Paul II said:

> The Bible itself speaks to us of the origin of the universe and its makeup, not in order to provide us with a scientific treatise

but in order to state the correct relationships of humanity with God and with the universe. Sacred Scripture wishes simply to declare that the world was created by God, and in order to teach this truth it expresses itself in the terms of the cosmology in use at the time of the writer. . . . Any other teaching about the origin and makeup of the universe is alien to the intentions of the Bible, which does not wish to teach us how heaven goes but how one goes to heaven. ("The Creation Story of Genesis," in *Catholic Update*, June 1994)

What Does the Church Teach About Heaven and Hell?

Clement Chee
Strake Jesuit College Preparatory, Houston, Texas

As a fifteen-year-old, I do not usually think or talk about death. For me, heaven and hell can wait. There are times, however, when things happen, such as natural disasters, the death of a relative, or news reports of soldiers dying, that make me think about what happens when we die.

Most of the time when someone mentions heaven or hell, the image that comes to mind is a place where people go when they die. Though traditionally imaged as places, heaven and hell are better pictured as states of being. Heaven is the state of being in which those who followed the Commandments and the Beatitudes receive the reward promised by Jesus Christ—eternal life with God the Father. Hell is the opposite of heaven. In hell are those who purposely separated themselves from God here on earth.

What has helped me recently is to see heaven and hell as not only states to come but also as states that presently exist. I can and do experience heaven (or hell) now. Through what I say and do, I am helping bring forth the Kingdom of God "on earth as it is in heaven." By not bringing God's will to our lives, we make it more like hell, which is the opposite of what God wants for us.

What Does the Church Teach About War?

Candice Norrell
Saint Mary's University, Winona, Minnesota

This question is of particular interest to me as I have grown up in a military family. My father has been deployed overseas for Operation Desert Shield, Operation Desert Storm, and Operation Iraqi Freedom, and he will be going back to Iraq again within another year's time. I also have friends who are in the military, have gone to war, and have died in war.

These are the seven classic conditions of a just war:

- There must be just cause. (That is, war is being used to correct a grave, public evil).
- The right authority must declare war. (Congress is the only authority in the United States permitted to declare war. Not even the president can do that on his own.)
- There must be hope of success.
- The right means must be used. (This means no nuclear bombs and so on. This doesn't mean there won't be damage to nearby buildings; it means the margin of error is reduced drastically.)
- There must be sufficient proportion between good and evil. The overall destruction expected from the use of force must be outweighed by the good to be achieved.
- It must be the last resort.
- There must be right intention. War may be used for a truly just cause and for that cause only.

If any of these conditions are not met, a war cannot be considered just, and Catholics should not participate.

Some people differ on how to apply just-war norms in particular cases, especially when events are moving rapidly and the facts are not altogether clear. This was particularly true in regard to the recent war in Iraq. Yet the Church teaches that all people and all governments must do everything they can to avoid war. Our faith tells us it makes more sense to resolve conflicts without using violence.

What Does the Term *Consistent Ethic of Life* Mean?

Samuel P. Thompson
Saint Thomas High School, Houston, Texas

Pope John Paul II continually referred to the ongoing issue of society's being immersed in and accepting of a "culture of death." To understand this in the context of the commandment "Thou shall not kill," one must see the culture of death as something that contradicts God's own mandate to humanity and as inconsistent with recognizing the basic human dignity of all people from womb to tomb—in other words, a consistent ethic of life.

Pope John Paul II often spoke out against the proliferation of violence in the world; a violence he had become all too familiar with during World War II in war-ravaged Poland. He sought peaceful resolution and enjoined his fellow Poles to rally as one in solidarity—in communion with one another against the Russian Socialist regime. He spoke out on behalf of convicted criminals sentenced to death and was a vehement opponent of abortion, contraception, and euthanasia. He reminded us that human life is sacred and that we have a duty to protect and foster it at all stages of development—from conception to natural death—and in all circumstances.

Pope John Paul II modeled this when he visited the man who had attempted to assassinate him. The Pope reached out in forgiveness and reconciliation, leading by his own example. He showed that we must not confuse justice with retaliation or vengeance; we must not confuse the quality of life with productivity, physical attraction, good or bad behavior, or some unspoken standard of convenience.

What Happens When We Sin?

Peter Nguyen
Saint Martha High School, Kennebunk, Maine

When we choose to do wrong instead of good, we commit sin and we hurt our relationships with ourselves, with others, and with God. Sin is any word we speak, action we perform, or deliberate thought we have that is contrary to the laws of God. When we sin, we reject God's will for us to be good. When we sin, we are choosing to not follow the way of Jesus, who was obedient to God in all things.

Often many of us are unaware of the seriousness of our sins. For example, there could be a time when a person might break one of the Ten Commandments, such as "Thou shall not steal." We all know that people are not supposed to take what is not theirs, but they sometimes do. I have stolen things before, and I have learned that it's wrong. I realized that by sinning in this way, I was not only harming myself but also hurting others by taking things that did not belong to me.

Though it may seem like most sins hurt only the sinner, even the most private of acts have social dimensions. If you take the time to think about any type of sin, you can easily begin to see how it can affect not only the person who commits it but also the relationships that person has with others and with God.

When we sin, the Church calls us to recognize our failings and make things right. Through Jesus the Church offers us opportunities to redeem and improve our lives, as we are always a work in progress.

Why Does There Sometimes Seem to Be an Inconsistency Between What I Say I Believe and What I Actually Do?

Emilee Burns
Gibault Catholic High School, Waterloo, Illinois

Have you ever said to yourself, "I can't believe I just did that?" Well, I have. It's not that I'm a horrible person, but there have been times when I have done things that weren't reflective of who I am.

I always smile when I hear someone say that being a Christian is easy. In all my eighteen years, when I take Jesus seriously, the last thing that following Jesus is . . . is easy. In fact, I think there ought to be a warning given to us at Baptism: We expect you to take this seriously and live it.

When I look at Jesus, I see the ideal meeting the real. Not only is he fully divine, but he is the fullness of what it means to be human.

However, I'm still in process. But I think I'm moving in the right direction. I'm active in school, I participate in extracurriculars, and I even have time to relate to my family. It goes without saying though—I'm busy. I think this is where the inconsistencies come in. With time being what it is, sometimes I'll try to take a shortcut. Being in relationship with Jesus demands time and attention. When I don't give this relationship attention, other things, which aren't always the best for me, come into my life.

One thing that helps me bridge the gap between who I say I am and what I actually do is weekly Mass. It's the one time of the week when I hear Jesus clearly say to me, "Come, follow me." I look around. I see friends and neighbors who, like me, are struggling to be more like Jesus. With the support of a faith-filled community, it is a bit easier to say yes to Jesus's invitation to be his disciple. The tension between what I say I believe and what I actually do doesn't leave, but at least I'm owning the tension.

Teens Share Their
Understanding **of Jesus**

What Do *Fully Human* **and** *Fully Divine* **Mean?**

Kevin Fox
Xavier High School, New York, New York

Jesus as "fully human" means that Jesus lived like us on earth in every way, except he did not sin. As Catholics we believe that in the person of Jesus, God became a human being, and one like us, in order to show us who God is and how we should live our lives.

When we think of Jesus as fully human, we tend to focus on his teachings and how he lived his life up to and including the events surrounding his death. Similarly, Jesus struggled with temptations and had doubts about his faith, just as we do today.

Jesus as "fully divine" is also at the core of a Catholic's faith, but it is more difficult to describe. Catholics believe Jesus is divine and one with God since the beginning of time. One of the reasons we believe Jesus is fully divine is because he was resurrected from the dead. Through this we proclaim him as our Lord and Savior.

We can better understand Jesus as fully divine by looking at the many miracles he performed during his ministry. Jesus healed many who were crippled or suffered from leprosy, blindness, and other physical and mental illnesses and ailments. Jesus's divinity is also shown through the many encounters he had with people after his Resurrection.

The terms *fully human* and *fully divine* refer to a Catholic's understanding of the nature of Jesus. Our beliefs about Jesus's humanity and divinity are clearly stated in the Nicene Creed.

Did Jesus Struggle and Feel Emotions the Way We Do?

Hope Olexa
Saint Francis Catholic High School, Gainesville, Florida

Like all humans, Jesus made mistakes. But like God, Jesus did not sin. There's a big difference between imperfection and sinfulness. The fact that Jesus was fully human allows us to understand Jesus better and shows us how to handle our own imperfections.

When Jesus was twelve years old, he ventured from Nazareth to Jerusalem with his family and friends to the Passover festival. When the group returned home, Jesus stayed in the Temple, unbeknownst to his parents. Mary and Joseph thought he was with the group heading back to Nazareth. After a day's walk, they realized Jesus was missing and panicked. Mary and Joseph searched frantically and found Jesus back at the Temple.

Mary questioned him: "Child, why have you treated us like this? Look, your father and I have been searching for you in great anxiety" (Luke 2:48). Jesus calmly pointed out: "Why were you searching for me? Did you not know that I must be in my Father's house?" (Luke 2:49). This bewildered Mary and Joseph. With the immaturity of a twelve-year-old child, Jesus did not contemplate the consequences of his actions.

Jesus, like most other people, also got angry. Later in life, during his public ministry, he went inside the Jerusalem Temple. There he saw people selling goods and making a convenience store out of a sacred dwelling. This infuriated him, so he harshly threw out the vendors and knocked over their goods (see Mark 11:15–17). Like Jesus, sometimes when we get angry, we lose control. Displays of emotion, even strong ones, are not always acts of sin but demonstrations of our humanity.

The word *perfection* doesn't so much describe what Jesus does or how he does it, but rather why he does it. This can be said in one word: *love.* Betrayed by friends and feeling abandoned by God, he utters from the cross, "My God, my God, why have you forsaken me?" (Mark 15:34). In the face of death, Jesus has a very human response. Yet, in order to bring about the salvation of the world, he offers his life for the redemption of all creation, saying, "Father, into your hands I commend my spirit" (Luke 23:46).

Did Jesus Have Any Brothers or Sisters?

Will Gordon
Pope John Paul II High School, Hendersonville, Tennessee

The question of whether Jesus actually had siblings is complex, confusing, and, at times, controversial. The Catholic Church teaches that Jesus was in fact an only child.

Though there are numerous instances in the New Testament where "brothers" and "sisters" of the Lord are mentioned, it is helpful to note that the term *brother* had a varied meaning in biblical times. During the time of Christ, the term was not restricted to the literal meaning of what we now understand to be a full brother or half brother. The same goes for *sister.* Many argue that the children in Jesus's home were actually Joseph's from a previous marriage. Another suggestion is that Jesus's brethren, his brothers and sisters, were actually cousins.

Emphasizing the Scriptures, many Christians have chosen to answer the question of whether Jesus had brothers and sisters in the affirmative. People with a literalist bent toward the Sacred Scriptures could make this conclusion. However, such a conclusion is contrary not only to a thorough understanding of the Sacred Scriptures but also Sacred Tradition. The most common reference to Jesus's siblings is in the story of Jesus's returning to his own country. In Mark 6:3, the people in the synagogue ask, "Is not this the carpenter, the son of Mary and brother of James and Joses and Judas and Simon, and are not his sisters here with us?" By Mark's record, Jesus had at least six siblings—four brothers and two sisters. Also, on two accounts, the Gospel of John mentions the family of Jesus. The first account is John 2:12. This passage mentions that Jesus went to Capernaum with his mother, his brothers, and his disciples. The second mention is in John 7:3–4. Here it states that Jesus's brothers advised him to go to Judea and show his disciples his works, for they did not believe him.

Finally, at the foot of the cross, Jesus tells Mary, speaking of John, "Woman, here is your son" (John 19:26). Jesus would not have entrusted Mary to John's care had he had brothers and sisters to take her in. These comments are in keeping with the Church's teaching that Mary was "ever virgin."

The Catholic Church maintains that Mary had only one child, Jesus, who was not biologically the son of Joseph. After the birth of our Lord, no mention is made of Mary and Joseph's ever having other children. Never do the Scriptures refer to the "sons of Mary" or "a son of Mary," but only "*the* son of Mary."

Was Jesus *Really* Jewish?

Tara Hollinshead
Gibault Catholic High School, Waterloo, Illinois

Jesus was born of a Jewish mother in Galilee, a Jewish part of the world. All of his family, friends, and disciples were Jews. We know that Jesus regularly worshiped in the synagogue and preached from a Jewish text (see Luke 4:14–21). He celebrated the Jewish festivals. The New Testament includes numerous references to Jesus's being a devout Jew. For instance, the Book of Hebrews tells us that "it is evident that our Lord was descended from Judah" (7:14). Both a Samaritan woman and the Roman governor Pontius Pilate clearly recognized that Jesus was Jewish (see John 4:9 and 18:35).

Tragically, at times throughout history (the Holocaust in particular), Christians have forgotten this central aspect of Jesus. We must never forget though.

In this context, it is important to remember that what we call Christianity did not come about until after Jesus's death. Still, the belief that Jesus was in fact a Jew is foundational for the Church's, and our own, understanding of Jesus.

What's All the Controversy About *The Da Vinci Code* and Jesus?

Samuel P. Thompson
Saint Thomas High School, Houston, Texas

Since it was published (and then made into a motion picture), Dan Brown's novel *The Da Vinci Code* has created a tremendous amount of controversy in the literary and religious communities of the world. The center of this furor focuses on suggestions that Jesus and Mary Magdalene were married, that there were suppressed Gospels, and that a political manipulation of Christianity by the Church hierarchy existed from the time of Constantine and continues even today.

Brown successfully creates a work of fiction, juxtaposing authentic circumstances and locations with an historic backdrop. Instead of reading an exciting novel that captures the imagination and allows one to escape into a seemingly harmless plot, a reader could be persuaded to accept the author's assertions as revealed and enlightened truth.

By misrepresenting critical pieces of information about the life of Christ, the Resurrection, and Church organizations, this work of fiction distorts history to confuse, confound, and sensationalize a

Hollywood storyline. The novel is seen by some as a means to capitalize on emotional, hot-button topics designed to provoke doubt and shake the faith of believers, while at the same time reaffirming the disbelief and simmering anger of those seeking to disavow and disengage from the institution of Church.

For some, the conspiracy-driven motives of Brown's storyline raise doubts regarding the integrity of Church Tradition, religious institutions, and the authority of the Magisterium (the teaching arm of the Church).

In response to the book's popularity, the Church has sought to provide information to those who have questions about Jesus Christ and Christian origins. Whether describing the celibacy of Jesus, the divinity of Christ, the image of Opus Dei, the role of women in the Church, or the suppression of some Gospels, Brown's understanding differs markedly from what the Catholic Church teaches.

What Was Jesus's Relationship with Women Like?

Margaret Lavinghousez
Saint James Cathedral, Orlando, Florida

Jesus did not exclude women from his ministry and always preached to and through women, even though, in Jesus's time, women were low on the totem pole—above slaves but below men.

Jesus ignored these social barriers and spoke, preached, and befriended any woman who would listen. The woman at the well (see John 4:1–42) was an example of his blindness to socioeconomic position. The woman was completely taken aback when Jesus, a male Jew, spoke to her, a Samaritan woman. Samaritans were considered lower than Jews because they were not of pure Jewish heritage. Nevertheless, Jesus spoke to her about his "living water," and, in turn, the woman told the people of her town about the wonders of Jesus's "water." The Gospel goes on to say that because of the woman's testimony, the entire town believed in Jesus's message.

Jesus also cured women and then invited them into his ministry. Mary Magdalene was one such woman (see Luke 8:2). Jesus cast the demons from her, saving her both physically and spiritually. She followed him, witnessed his miracles, and listened to his teachings. She would eventually become one of his closest disciples. She was present at his Crucifixion and was the first to witness his Resurrection.

Jesus defended women as well. When the adulteress was about to be stoned, Jesus called out to the rock-holding crowd: "You sin, she sins, and you have no right to judge!" (see John 8:1–11). He also defended the woman who washed his feet with her tears (see Luke 7:36–39). The disciples wanted to throw her out, but Jesus allowed her to wash and anoint his feet, and then he forgave and blessed her for her faith.

Jesus knew and loved how faithful, passionate, and strong women are, and he understood their place on earth and in heaven. The modern Church has recognized this truth and believes that old cultural and religious standards, which do not credit women as equal inheritors of the Kingdom through Christ, should be abandoned. How could such a truth be denied when a woman was granted one of the holiest and most awesome positions in history—to give birth to the Messiah?

What Was John the Baptist's Connection with Jesus?

Kaley Dyan Matthews
Christian Brothers High School, Sacramento, California

John the Baptist and Jesus had a special connection from the time they were both born. Their mothers, Elizabeth and Mary, were related, and it is said that John and Jesus were cousins. Besides a familial connection though, there are far greater spiritual ones.

In the Gospels, John the Baptist appears as a prophet, calling the people of Israel to penance. This is symbolized in his practice of baptism in order to prepare for the coming Messiah. John made it clear to those who asked, however, that he was not the Messiah: "I baptize with water. Among you stands one whom you do not know, the one who is coming after me; I am not worthy to untie the thong of his sandal" (John 1:26–28).

Hearing of John's ministry, Jesus traveled to the Jordan River to see him. There Jesus was baptized by John in the Jordan. After this Jesus began his public ministry, proclaiming the Kingdom of God.

Jesus once asked his disciples who people thought he was: "Who do people say that I am?" (Mark 8:27). One of them replied, "John the Baptist" (Mark 8:28). This, of course, was not the right answer, but it gives us a sense of the link people saw between the two. About John, Jesus would say, "Truly I tell you, among those born of women no one has arisen greater than John the Baptist" (Matthew 11:11). So, in both life and death, there was a connection between them.

While John the Baptist's ministry was characterized by a life of self-denial, Jesus's ministry manifested a love of relationship with people as seen in his table fellowship with a variety of people (see Matthew 11:16–19).

Interestingly, both John the Baptist and Jesus met similar fates. For his public criticism of Herod Antipas, John eventually had his head cut off (see Mark 6:17–29). Some years later, Jesus was publicly crucified for being a threat to both the religious and state establishments.

Why Did Jesus Die? Who Killed Him?

Carlos Galletti
Xavier High School, New York, New York

This question can be answered by reading the Passion narratives found in the Gospels of Mark (chapters 14–15), Matthew (chapters 26–27), Luke (chapters 22–23), and John (chapters 18–19).

Jesus died on the cross for us because he knew our world was filled with sin. During his time here on earth, he managed to save us and form a foundation for his Church. He gave himself to be crucified so that humans could live. This is the ultimate selfless act of Jesus.

The Scriptures tell us that "[Christ] himself bore our sins in his body on the cross, so that, free from sins, we might live for righteousness; by his wounds you have been healed" (1 Peter 2:24). Salvation from sin and death for every person in every age comes through the death and Resurrection of Jesus Christ.

In a historical context, there is significance in noting that Jesus died by Crucifixion. The Romans crucified only those who were slaves or revolutionaries. In other words, Jesus challenged those who exercised political, economic, and religious power. Crucifixion was propaganda used by the Romans to say to others, "Don't do what he did!"

Though some high-profile Jewish officials were involved in the death of Jesus, it is inexcusable and unacceptable to blame all Jews then and now as responsible for his death.

Why Did Jesus Say, "My God, My God, Why Have You Forsaken Me?" from the Cross?

Ian Bozant
Notre Dame High School, Sherman Oaks, California

"At three o'clock Jesus cried out with a loud voice, 'Eloi, Eloi, lema sabachthani?' which means, 'My God, my God, why have you forsaken me?'" (Mark 15:34). Here we see in the midst of the great Paschal mystery, the victory over Satan and death, the glorious fulfillment of the messianic prophecies. We see something that seems terribly out of place; we see doubt! We see our Savior's crying out to God the Father in a voice we can imagine only as distressed and deeply pained. So if this is a great victory, then why is Jesus seemingly in a state of defeat or despair? The answer is simple: This is one of the times in the Bible where Jesus shows us his human nature. Christ cried out because he was human and was feeling the weight of our sins and the weight of the cross. He was dying an excruciatingly painful death while atoning for every one of humanity's sins and conquering the power of hell.

Jesus's lament on the cross should serve as a source of comfort to humanity, as it shows that Jesus did feel the same pains and despairs we feel each and every day. It shows us that Jesus is truly "one of us," in the sense that he was not immune to pain and suffering because he was the Son of God. In his cry from the cross, Jesus shows us that even he had doubts, but his faith never failed him, and he illustrates that our faith will never fail if we call out to God. Can you imagine the Blessed Mother, Mary Magdalene, John, and the other believers when Jesus died, with his last words being doubtful? They must have been terrified! Their faith was strong, but seeing their Savior in such a state must have shaken them. This is important because these were the first members of the Church, and we carry on their roles in the Church today. When Jesus was resurrected, they became certain his words of doubt were of little significance to the battle over death.

Jesus gave us hope in his last words and in his Resurrection. We should look at these words and smile or be relieved because they represent for us our own lives. Jesus conquered his expression of doubt, and so can we. We can conquer the doubts of our faith through the help of Christ and through our own efforts to find him.

What Can I Do to Grow Closer to Jesus?

Emily Rose Elmo McLaughlin
Purcell Marian High School, Cincinnati, Ohio

Sometimes the schedules of my parents and older siblings cause my younger brothers to get overlooked or dragged around from place to place. They are pretty good at finding things to do, but some nights when Mom and Dad are gone, I end up putting them to bed. They look to me to be nice to them, to read or tell them a story, to give them a snack, or to laugh and play with them. I think my choice to love them, to take care of them, and to spend extra time with them is also a choice to grow closer to Jesus. When we reach out to others in loving and kind ways, we grow closer to Christ. We can also grow closer to Jesus by reading the Scriptures and taking time for private and personal prayer.

Another way to get closer to Jesus is by going to Mass on Sunday. Worshiping with a community reminds us of how Jesus would sit around the table and share meals with different people. When I look around the church, I see many different people. There's the man who coached my basketball team for years, my friends from grade school, my Girl Scout leaders, my old babysitter and her mother, and the older woman with a beautiful smile who always sits near the front. We are all brought together by Jesus. These are the people who know me, who have been a part of my growing up. This is the community where Jesus can be seen and felt and heard. When we gather with the community, we grow closer to Jesus.

How Is Reincarnation Different from Resurrection?

Ian Bozant
Notre Dame High School, Sherman Oaks, California

The Resurrection of Jesus Christ is the means by which we have received our salvation. It is the ultimate victory, as Jesus has conquered sin and death by rising to new life. This one incident is so important to our faith that without it, Christianity would not exist. For this reason, it is important that we, as Catholics, understand the Resurrection of Jesus as best we can.

One common misconception of the Resurrection is that it is similar to reincarnation. Reincarnation is a very different concept that should not be confused with the Resurrection. Reincarnation is the belief that when a person dies, he or she is born again into another body. This may be in the form of another human being or in the form of an animal. Reincarnation is believed to be a cycle of life, a cycle of rebirths. This belief is common in many Eastern religions, including Hinduism and Buddhism.

Resurrection stresses the belief the Jesus was raised from the dead—body and soul—so that we might have eternal life with him in heaven. In his Resurrection, Jesus was not merely born again into a new cycle of life. He broke free from the grasps of death and gave humanity a way to live eternally in everlasting happiness and peace in Christ. After we die, we too await our own bodily resurrection and union with God in heaven. In this sense, resurrection emphasizes that the only life we have is this one and that we must make the most of it.

Do Catholics Believe in Miracles?

Bart Thompson
Saint John's Jesuit High School, Toledo, Ohio

With scientific breakthroughs occurring every day, some people have begun to doubt whether the miracles Jesus performed were real. Some wonder if God intervenes in the world at all anymore as God did in the times of Jesus and the prophets. Were Jesus's miracles real then? Do miracles happen now?

Catholics believe that Jesus's miracles did in fact occur as described in the Gospels. The Catholic and Christian faith is built upon the belief that Jesus defied death and rose again to life, a miracle in itself. The miracles show that Jesus had power over all creation.

Still people ask about God's involvement in today's world. Sometimes we as Catholics may wonder if God is an acting force in our world today. Many people continue to experience miracles. It is important to have faith and to remember that God promised to always be with us and to always love us and guide our lives. Often the difference between a coincidental event and a supernatural one is in the eye of the beholder.

God miraculously intervened in my life shortly after a personal tragedy. A few days before the start of high school, one of my best friends died after being hit by a truck. I entered a new school completely devastated. In the second week of school, my theology class went down to the chapel for a time of prayer and meditation. During this time, I fell into a relaxed state of prayer. In my mind, I saw Jesus on the hill. I approached him and asked him if my friend was okay. We talked about all the pain her death caused me. I prayed she'd be alright. Suddenly I felt a soft breeze on my neck, as if someone was blowing on it. My eyes flew open, and I looked around; no one was anywhere near me. I believe that was God's breath helping to ease my heart and let me know my friend was alright.

What Is the Second Coming?

Jordan Shipley
Cathedral High School, Indianapolis, Indiana

The Second Coming, as it is understood by the Church, is the day on which Christ will gloriously return to earth. It's also referred to as the Parousia (Greek for "return"). This will include a judgment of humanity and all of creation.

An image of the Second Coming is found in the Gospel of Matthew. The disciples approach Jesus on the Mount of Olives, wondering what will happen to humanity at the end of the world. Christ emphasizes two main points in his explanation. First, we as humans know neither the day nor the hour at which Christ will return (see Matthew 24:36). He might reappear tomorrow or two thousand years from now. In any case, Christ must find us ready. The early members of the Church took this message to heart. They believed that Jesus's return would be soon after his death and Resurrection, and consequently they lived each day in the love of God and the service of others, as we ourselves should.

At the Second Coming, Christ will separate those who have followed his will from those who have not. Every person will be held accountable for her or his own deeds. Those who have followed Christ will be welcomed into God's eternal, heavenly Kingdom. Those who have failed to follow Christ will be sent to eternal punishment. At the end of time, the Kingdom of God will come into its perfection.

The second point to understand is that the end will not be easy (see Matthew 24:3–31). Christ somberly informed his Apostles that the earth's final days will be dark and dangerous. Nations will rise up against one another. Christians will undergo intense persecution. False prophets will arise, and many will be deceived and betray their faith. The great powers of the world will fall. Natural disasters of mythic proportions will strike the face of the earth. The love of many will grow cold. This being said, we have to be careful not to view every tragedy or event as a sign of the impending end.

The Church reassures us of the constancy of Christ's love. His love will never leave us, and because of this, we will have the strength to endure anything in the world. Christ will arrive in glory at his Second Coming and, if we are prepared, we will live with him for all eternity.

What and Who Is the Antichrist?

Zachary Futterer
Joliet Catholic Academy, Joliet, Illinois

Throughout the centuries, the ominous figure of the Antichrist has taunted both believers and nonbelievers into a mindset of fear and anxiety. Numerous novels have been written and movies made that profit from society's interest in and confusion about the Antichrist.

We can find a concise definition of the Antichrist in the Scriptures: "Who is the liar but the one who denies that Jesus is the Christ? This is the antichrist, the one who denies the Father and the Son" (1 John 2:22). Rather than some larger-than-life figure, here the Antichrist is seen as someone who teaches false doctrine or is no longer practicing the faith. In this case, though we may believe that the Antichrist is still to appear, John says that many such figures have already lived.

Many people connect the Book of Revelation with the Antichrist. In Revelation we get images of the beast, the dragon, and the whore of Babylon. However, we must remember that the Book of Revelation is a type of apocalyptic literature. Apocalyptic literature is written to sound like an attempt to foretell the future by using symbols and visions. But the symbols are often codes for people and events in the present.

A better sense of the Antichrist is to be found in understanding it as a symbol of the power and presence of evil. Sometimes this power and presence can become personified in one person—the Antichrist. (Conjectures to actual historical persons being the Antichrist have proven unsuccessful.)

The best thing to do is to model our lives on the person of Jesus. If we do that, the Antichrist hasn't got a chance.

3 Teens Share Their Understanding of the Scriptures

What Does It Mean When We Say the Bible Is Inspired and Inerrant?

David Rudy

Lancaster Catholic High School, Lancaster, Pennsylvania

The Bible, the word of God, is both inspired and inerrant, meaning that God is the divine author of the Bible and that the Bible is free from error in matters of truth, or all matters that relate to our salvation.

The origin and source of the Bible is God, not the human authors. However, God did not simply dictate the words of the Bible to its writers; instead the Holy Spirit guided and moved the authors to reveal God's message. All Christians believe that God is the ultimate author of the Bible because the Holy Spirit inspired the human authors in their writing. But some Christians, sometimes called fundamentalists or literalists, believe that every part of the Bible is absolutely true in every way. Catholics believe that the inspired word is meant to teach humanity about God and God's expectations of how every person should live.

Catholics believe that the Bible cannot be taken literally in the strictest sense, for its messages would sometimes appear to be in conflict. For example, Jesus preaches to cut off a body part if it causes a human to sin (see Mark 9:43–48), whereas Saint Paul teaches that man's body is sacred and a temple of the Holy Spirit (see 1 Corinthians 6:19).

It can be dangerous to rely too heavily on the literal meaning of the Bible's words. The underlying message is infinitely more important. By saying the Bible is inerrant, the Church acknowledges that all the messages and themes of the Bible related to our salvation agree with God's teachings and are free from error. In some cases, the Bible is not historically or scientifically correct, and details or even entire stories may never have occurred, such as the story of Adam and Eve or of Noah's taking animals onto an ark for forty days. However, the message is what is important: Adam and Eve represent humanity's flawed nature and downfall, and Noah and the ark reveal disaster for the immoral and wicked and salvation for the just and faithful.

What Is the Difference Between a Catholic Bible and a Protestant Bible?

David Loeffler
Yuma Catholic High School, Yuma, Arizona

The main differences between a Catholic Bible and a Protestant Bible can be found in the books of Wisdom, Sirach, Judith, Baruch, Tobit, 1 Maccabees, 2 Maccabees, and additions to the Books of Esther and Daniel. Simply put, Catholics include these books in their canon (official list) of Scripture, whereas Protestants do not. Catholics call these seven books the Deuterocanonical books; Protestants call them the Apocrypha (Greek for "hidden").

As the Church formed the canon of the Bible (the list of books considered "inspired"), the Old Testament portion of the canon was taken from the Septuagint. The Septuagint is the name of the original Greek translation of the Old Testament used by Diaspora Jews (those who lived outside the Holy Land) and early Christians. We know this because at the time, Greek was the common language of the Mediterranean world, and the Hebrew language was dying. When the Jewish rabbis developed their canon and eventually finalized it, it had all the same books as the Greek Septuagint with the exception of the seven books named earlier. They decided not to include those seven books because they did not have Hebrew versions of them.

In the 1500s, the Protestant reformers followed Martin Luther in deciding to go with the Jewish rabbis and delete the seven Deuterocanonical books from the canon. Since then we have had two Christian bibles: the Catholic Bible, with forty-six books, and the Protestant Bible, with thirty-nine.

This being said, both Catholics and Protestants value the Bible as the revealed word of God. The revelation of Jesus found within it is shared by all of us.

Is There Anything I Should Know About Interpreting the Bible Before I Begin Reading It?

Patrick E. Perez
Archbishop McCarthy High School, Fort Lauderdale, Florida

The Bible is not historical or scientific writing. Just because something may not be literally true in a historical or scientific sense (the story of Adam and Eve, for example) doesn't mean it lacks value. It simply means we must seek the deeper meaning, its religious truth. One way we do this is by being attentive to what the authors intended to say and to what God wanted to reveal. In other words, we must try to relate the passages to our own lives.

Whether reading the Old or New Testament, we should ask ourselves how each passage relates to Jesus. When reading the Bible, it is sometimes helpful to look for the similarities among the people and stories and see how they can relate to Jesus and how they can help us become better Catholics. In other words, relating the passages to our own lives can help us grow in faith and help us get to know God through Jesus the Christ and the workings of the Holy Spirit.

Another good principle to use when reading the Bible is to read it in a "holistic" sense. Rather than getting caught up in one passage or verse, such as one that advocates war, we should consider what all the Scriptures teach about war (especially Jesus's teachings).

Catholics believe that everything in the Bible related to our salvation is true, although not all of it happened as described. This may seem a bit confusing, but we must see some of the stories in the Bible as analogies for Jesus. By reading the Bible in a Christological sense, we are able to better understand the greatest gift God has ever given us—his Son, Jesus. As Catholics, it is our responsibility to appreciate the book of God and use it to better recognize God.

What Are Some of the Most Important Themes of the Scriptures?

Annika Gunderson
Cotter High School, Winona, Minnesota

The two greatest themes of the Scriptures are covenant and love. In the Hebrew Scriptures, the Book of Genesis contains stories of God's establishing a covenant of love with all creation and, by our refusal to honor it, the effects of sin. This is dramatically seen in the stories of Adam and Eve, Cain and Abel, and Noah. These references make it clear that Satan (or selfishness) is constantly tempting us, trying to push our consciences and hearts away from God's covenant.

With all this pressure, and because humans are far from perfect, it is easy for us to fall into sin's deceits. This may leave us feeling guilty, even shameful. But we must always remember that God forgives and absolves. When we address our feelings with God and express our sorrow, God will in turn forgive. It is crucial to recognize that God's gift of grace eternally overpowers sin.

The theme of love is strongly emphasized in the New Testament. Love is more than just an emotional connection between two people.

It is the most powerful gift from God. This is evident in the Incarnation—God's becoming human.

God gives us the power of love in order for us to multiply it. When others have been touched by this gift, they then can pass it on, thus making that beautiful process a contagious, regenerating cycle. It is said in 1 Corinthians 13:8 that "love never ends." Although many other elements of our lives will someday end, the legacy and manifestation of love eternally remain. This proves true by our acts of faith, which may be unseen or unheard though never without meaning.

Without ever taking the chance of opening our hearts to as many people—both friends and enemies—as possible during our lives, we are underestimating one of the most wondrous, influential assets God empowered our spirits with. As it says in First Corinthians, "And now faith, hope, and love abide, these three; and the greatest of these is love" (13:13).

Is the Creation Story of Genesis Meant to Be Taken Literally?

Erik Sheets
Saint Xavier High School, Cincinnati, Ohio

The Book of Genesis actually has two different Creation stories in its first chapters. The Catholic Church teaches that Genesis was written as a symbolic story (also called a mythic story) to convey great moral and spiritual truths. We should not try to come to any scientific conclusions about the Creation of the world from reading these stories. Catholics believe that God created the world and everything in it but do not believe the world was created in literally six twenty-four-hour days. The important thing isn't about what God created when, as some Christians want to emphasize. They take the Creation story of Genesis as scientific and historical fact.

As we continue to figure out more about how the world came to be, more spiritual mysteries remain, and this is where we can find God.

The Book of Genesis, though it may not give an accurate scientific explanation of our Creation, does give us a mystery to think about in terms of who God actually is and what God's big plan is. Most important, we must always recognize that God created everything out of love and that all Creation is sacred.

What Exactly Is a Fundamentalist?

Ian Bozant
Notre Dame High School, Sherman Oaks, California

The Bible is one of the roots of our Catholic faith. It contains the word of God and gives us direction on our lifelong journey toward the arms of Christ. This book (actually it is a collection of them) is so important because it is one of the primary ways of truly knowing what God wants from us and what we need to do in order to spend everlasting life with God in heaven. Therefore, it is important that we understand how to read the Bible and interpret its messages. This is where we Catholics differ from fundamentalist Christians.

Fundamentalists are followers of Christ who believe that the Bible is the inspired word of God and who believe in its literal interpretation and fundamental teachings. Fundamentalists feel that the Bible needs no interpretation and that the words of the Scriptures are exactly what God meant for us to hear and know.

The Catholic Church, however, teaches us that the words of the Bible were inspired by the work of the Holy Spirit. As such, we must read and interpret them in light of the same Spirit who inspired the authors of these sacred texts. We must take into account the authors' intentions, the culture of the time period, and the literary techniques used to convey and capture the audience.

My Friend Said That to Be Saved, You Have to Be Born Again. What Does That Mean?

Chris Johnson

Saint Pius X High School, Houston, Texas

Protestants who believe in being "born again" take the idea from the story of Nicodemus found in the Gospel of John (see 3:1–21). In the story, Nicodemus asks Jesus what must happen before he can enter the Kingdom of heaven. Jesus tells Nicodemus that he must be born again, not meaning that Nicodemus's mother must bear him again, but that Nicodemus must truthfully believe in the Holy Spirit.

Some Protestants take this story literally, believing that they will have a life-changing conversion experience, usually during a powerful preacher's sermon. They will then be able to recite the day, place, and time they accepted Jesus as their personal savior.

Catholics do not say they were saved on a certain day. In fact, "being saved" is not a phrase Catholics use to express our relationship with Jesus. We are far more likely to say we were born anew in Baptism. We then spend the rest of our lives striving to journey with God. Protestants who are born again speak with great certainty that they have been saved, whereas Catholics are not certain of their salvation; rather, we stress the ongoing need for conversion celebrated first in Baptism. It's the journey, the long haul, that Catholics emphasize.

That being said, Catholics do profess a belief in Jesus Christ. In fact, every week while proclaiming the Nicene Creed, we say yes to belief in and relationship with Jesus.

What Are the Synoptic Gospels?

Rachel Irene Victoria Thompson

Saint Agnes Academy, Houston, Texas

Synoptic is a term used by Scripture scholars to refer to the Gospels according to Mark, Matthew, and Luke. The word *synoptic* is broken down into two parts: the prefix *syn* means "the same or similar," and *optic* is a word that refers to vision.

Literally translated then, *synoptic* means "seen with the same or similar vision." The term *synoptic* is used to compare the contents of these three Gospels as they are viewed side by side. The Gospels attributed to Matthew, Mark, and Luke can be seen together primarily recounting the same stories about Jesus of Nazareth, though they differ in length and some details.

The Gospel according to John differs significantly from Matthew, Mark, and Luke in content, style, and language and is therefore not included as one of the synoptic Gospels. John's Gospel is written much later and uses language rich in allegory, symbolism, and metaphor.

The consensus among Scripture scholars is that Mark was written first (around AD 65), followed by Matthew and Luke, both of which drew upon Mark's Gospel to frame their own.

Why Do Christians Use the Hebrew Scriptures?

Stephanie Brennan

Blessed Sacrament Church, Covington, Kentucky

The first reason Christians use the Hebrew Scriptures is because Jesus was Jewish. Jesus and his first disciples all shared this religious tradition. Their Scriptures were the Hebrew Scriptures, also known as the Old Testament. The Old Testament rituals and beliefs formed and shaped them.

In addition, much of the New Testament relates to the Hebrew Scriptures. For example, the Jews celebrated the first Passover by applying the blood of the lamb to their door mantel. This was a sign for the angel of death to "pass over" the household. Thus the blood of the lamb was the salvation for the Jews. In the New Testament, Jesus celebrates Passover with his Apostles when he gives them his body and blood in the Eucharist. Jesus is known as the Lamb of God. It is through the blood of the Lamb that the entire world is saved. Without knowing this event from the Hebrew Scriptures, we wouldn't be able to make sense of its reference to Jesus.

Furthermore, because of our familiarity with the Hebrew Scriptures, we better understand Jesus when he's referred to as the new Adam or new Moses. Also, in the infancy narrative of Matthew, when Jesus goes to Egypt to escape Herod, many commentators see here a parallel to the Jews' fleeing slavery.

The Hebrew Scriptures tell the history of the Jewish people. In them we see that salvation history begins with God's working with the Israelites. We see the history of our Savior, as Jesus was a Jew.

It goes without saying: The better we know the Hebrew Scriptures, the better we know Jesus. The Hebrew Scriptures belong to both Jewish and Christian believers.

What Is the Kingdom of God That Jesus Talks About?

Robert J. Gallic III
Delbarton School, Morristown, New Jersey

The notion of the Kingdom of God is one constantly referenced in the New Testament. John the Baptist urges his followers to "repent, for the kingdom of heaven has come near" (Matthew 3:2). Jesus takes a similar attitude: "Truly I tell you, whoever does not receive the kingdom of God as a little child will never enter it" (Mark 10:15). These two examples, among many from the Gospels, present two ideas of the Kingdom of God. In the first example, the Kingdom of God takes a physical, or earthly, nature, wheras the second example implies a spiritual state of being in union with God.

The physical and spiritual natures of the Kingdom of God are areas that overlap one another. In this Kingdom, justice and peace prevail. Until that Kingdom is established, however, Catholics have a sacred mission to cooperate with the workings of the Holy Spirit to help bring about the fulfillment of the Kingdom by building a just society where the dignity of every person is respected. This is why in the Lord's Prayer we pray, "Thy Kingdom come, thy will be done on earth as it is in heaven."

Another way of speaking of the Kingdom of God is to describe it in terms of present and future. We live in the Kingdom right now, but its full realization awaits us in heaven. So the Kingdom of God is an "already, but not yet" reality. Furthermore, as much as we speak about the Kingdom being a place, in another sense it is also about re-lationship. Where we find relationship—with others and with God—we find the Kingdom.

One way to accomplish this mission is to recognize the Kingdom of God in our hearts. God is always present to us, at every moment of our existence. We can reject this gift of God, or we can choose to have a relationship with God. When we do accept God, choosing to follow God's Commandments and God's will for our lives, the King-dom of God becomes manifested in our very beings.

The Holy Spirit dwells in our hearts, so we can say the Kingdom of God is within us. In the end, we have a choice every day of our lives whether to accept and build this Kingdom of God. It is up to us.

Why Did Jesus Use Parables?

Louis Murray

Gibault Catholic High School, Waterloo, Illinois

A parable is a literary form that uses a fictional story to make a point. Like most great teachers, Jesus wanted to challenge his followers to new ways of thinking and living. One of the qualities of a parable is its ability to make us think, to make us question our usual way of seeing the world. This is precisely why Jesus taught using parables—to help his followers see differently.

Two of the more memorable parables are that of the prodigal son (see Luke 15:11–32) and that of the good Samaritan (see Luke 10:25–37). In the first story, a son basically wishes his father dead by asking for his inheritance. The father gives the inheritance to him, and the son leaves and soon wastes the money on wine, women, and song. The shocking part of the parable comes when the son returns home. The father rushes out to greet him, embraces him, and clothes him, much to the frustration of the elder brother. The father then begins to prepare a great feast to welcome the lost son home. None of us are prepared for the father's unconditional love toward someone who now should be treated like a slave instead of a favored son. Such is the love of God. How often we fall short.

Our first clue that something unusual is going on in the story of the good Samaritan is the use of the word *good* in reference to a Samaritan. In Jesus's time, the one thing a Samaritan couldn't be was good. Jews and Samaritans hated each other. Yet when it comes time to aid a wounded traveler, who stops? It's not the people you'd expect—the priest, the Levite, or the scribe. It's the Samaritan. Think of someone you really dislike. Now picture that person helping you in your hour of greatest need. Here Jesus allows us to consider who our enemy and neighbor really is. This story has the potential, like all parables do, to make us uncomfortable.

This is what Jesus's parables do. They get us to expand our way of thinking and viewing the world. They challenge us to step outside the boxes we're in, to move beyond our comfort zones. By telling parables, Jesus allowed his message of guidance, wisdom, and understanding to survive the test of time.

Are There Any Lost Books of the Bible?

Dominic Schwab
Marian High School, Mishawaka, Indiana

In light of the bestselling book and movie *The Da Vinci Code*, there is much talk these days about lost books of the Bible. Among those in question are the Gospels of Thomas and Mary. These Gospels are referenced in *The Da Vinci Code* and have prompted people to go out and investigate them. Though *The Da Vinci Code* is an entertaining book and these "Gospels" do exist, they are not officially recognized parts of the Bible.

There are many legends of lost books, but there is no truth whatsoever to these stories. Every book that God intended and inspired to be in the Bible is in the Bible. There are literally hundreds of religious books that were written in the same time period as the books of the Bible. Some of these books contain true accounts of things that genuinely occurred. Some of them contain good spiritual teaching. However, these books are not believed by the Church to have been inspired by God.

How Did We Actually Get the New Testament When Jesus Never Wrote Down Anything?

Samantha Stempky

Cathedral High School, Indianapolis, Indiana

When people hear a really great story, usually the first thing they want to do is go tell it to someone else. This is what happened with Jesus's stories. Throughout his life on earth, Jesus spoke to many large groups of people, and specifically to the Apostles. After Jesus's death and Resurrection, the Apostles began evangelizing. They created faith communities and passed on Jesus's stories by word of mouth.

Oral tradition was a large part of ancient culture. It allowed history to be passed along from year to year until someone decided to write it down. This is exactly what happened with Jesus's teachings. As Christianity grew, however, some false teachings also began to emerge. Soon these contradictory ideas began to influence accounts of Jesus and his message. This made it even more important for the Church to write down the truth about Christ.

In an effort to fight back against the heresy, Christian writers began dictating the lessons of Jesus the Apostles had spread. Catholics believe that these writers were inspired by God, making God the true author. Through the years, these documents were translated into Greek, Latin, and eventually English.

How Should a Catholic Interpret the Book of Revelation?

Brandon Hines

Notre Dame High School, Sherman Oaks, California

When the rapture is brought up, many of us think of the end of the world, when everyone's very existence on earth comes to an end. The fiery pits of hell open up and envelop anyone not saved by the Second Coming of Jesus. As pictured in the media and popular culture, this is when Satan and all his evil cohorts ride through the earth on their chariots of fire, swallowing everything in their path. Those not saved are condemned to suffer for eternity in the bowels of hell, where they will endure torture and pain of the most unspeakable kind. Given this doomsday scenario, many people connect the rapture with the Book of Revelation, when in actuality, belief in this idea comes from Saint Paul (see 1 Thessalonians 4:17).

Pope John Paul II discouraged people from this way of thinking. In fact, when speaking of the end of time, rather than presenting an image of a Christ who condemns, the Church presents an image of a Savior who seeks to lead us into eternal life with his Father. For Catholics a God of love emerges, rather than a God who seeks to exact punishment and revenge for sin.

When interpreting the Book of Revelation (and the rest of the Bible for that matter), it is important to have some historical background. When Revelation was written (around AD 90), Christians were undergoing persecution by the Romans. The Book of Revelation is full of images and symbols. If we read the Book of Revelation literally, however, we miss the meaning and can come up with some "crazy" interpretations. Ultimately, the Book of Revelation is about the tension and struggle between being a believer in God and being a citizen of a country.

Why Does Saint Paul Have So Many Letters in the Bible?

Maria Schwab

Marian High School, Mishawaka, Indiana

Saint Paul has often been called the Apostle to the Gentiles. But if you look at a list of the twelve original Apostles, you will not find Saint Paul's name. An apostle is one who carries on Jesus's message and teachings. Saint Paul (earlier named Saul) had been a Jew who had persecuted Christians (or what might better be described as early Jewish followers of Jesus). Once he had his conversion on the road to Damascus (see Acts 26:4–23) though, he spent the rest of his life spreading the word of God. Toward the end of his life, in a reversal of roles, he himself was imprisoned for his faith in Jesus. Saint Paul wrote some of his letters while he was in prison.

Saint Paul made three missionary journeys to various parts of the Mediterranean world to share the story of Jesus with others. Some of the places he visited were Corinth, Ephesus, Thessalonica, Philippi, and Rome. Just as friends write letters to keep in touch with each other, Saint Paul wrote letters to the people in these cities, telling them what he had been doing and giving them advice on how to live as a follower of Christ. Some of his advice was about how to live morally. He also offered teachings on how communities were to worship and how people were to refrain from dissension and fighting within their community. These letters are Saint Paul's lasting legacy to the Church.

The New Testament includes thirteen letters written by Saint Paul, but many scholars believe that some of the letters traditionally attributed to Paul were actually written by associates or later followers. Without Saint Paul and all his letters, Christianity may have never left Jerusalem and become one of the major world religions today.

4 Teens Share Their Understanding **of the Mass (Liturgy) and the Sacraments**

What Does the "Real Presence" of Christ in the Eucharist Really Mean?

Dan Moore
Northridge Preparatory, Niles, Illinois

In the Eucharist, Jesus Christ is present in the fullest possible way. The Church speaks of other presences of Jesus Christ—in the assembly (where two or more are gathered), in the proclaimed word, and in the priest celebrating the liturgy.

Most especially, however, the Church teaches that Jesus Christ is present in the consecrated elements. The "real presence" means that Christ is present with his Body and Blood, under the appearances of bread and wine. At the moment of consecration during Mass, when the priest, acting in the person of Christ, says, "This is my body. . . . This is the cup of my blood" (*Sacramentary*, p. 545), the bread and wine change. The substances of bread and wine have been transformed by Christ's resurrected person.

The bread still tastes, feels, looks, and is in every exterior, observational way identical to bread, but its substance, its identity, what it *is*, has been replaced by the actual person of Jesus Christ. We call this process transubstantiation. This belief is one that separates Catholics from many other Christian traditions. But we have Jesus's own words to testify to this reality (see Matthew 26:26–29).

It is in the Eucharist that Christ's presence is most perfectly realized. The smallest particle of bread, the smallest droplet of wine that still can be identified as such, contains the whole Body and Blood of Jesus Christ.

Should I Go **to Mass If I'm Not Getting Anything Out of It?**

Rachel Irene Victoria Thompson
Saint Agnes Academy, Houston, Texas

Every time we buy a book, a magazine, a CD, or a ticket for a movie, we take a chance. For the most part, there will be something about our purchase we love and something we could live without. Mass is a little like this. Some days we don't want to be there, other times we enjoy being there, and still other times our families require us to be there. We can choose to sit and act bored or disinterested (wasting everyone's time), or we can make the most of it and choose to actively participate.

Many people believe they need to be entertained during Mass. But Mass is definitely not a spectator sport. We go to Mass to give of ourselves, not just to receive something. The Mass requires us to be actively engaged participants! By actively participating, we gain a deeper appreciation and understanding by giving a part of ourselves to the Mass and to those who are gathered to celebrate with us. This means we are attentive to the readings and join in with the responses and songs.

Even if we hear only one or two lines of Scripture, even if the priest says only one thing that catches our ears, even if we dislike the music, the Mass always offers us an opportunity to grow closer to God and the people of God. Participating in the Mass brings forgiveness for our sins and helps us resist further sin. In receiving the Eucharist, we are sent forth strengthened to be Christ's presence in the world.

Why Can't Those Who Are Not Catholic Receive Communion?

Jane M. Ryngaert

Saint Francis Catholic High School, Gainesville, Florida

It is customary in the Catholic Church that only Catholics receive the Eucharist during Mass. This is not meant as a form of discrimination against those who are not Catholic; rather, it is a tradition that originates from a difference in beliefs, and the Church has good reasons for not allowing this.

Catholics believe the bread and wine used in Communion actually become the Body and Blood of Jesus Christ. Most other Christian denominations believe that the bread and wine are simply symbols of Christ. In order for us to share the Eucharist together, we must first be united in belief.

When receiving the Eucharist in the Catholic Church, a priest or Eucharistic minister holds out the bread or wine and says, "The Body (or Blood) of Christ," to which the receiver replies, "Amen." By saying "Amen," the receiver is saying: "I believe. I believe that this *is* the actual Body and Blood of Jesus Christ."

The Catholic Church limits Communion to Catholics for this reason, to keep those who are not Catholic from making a false expression of faith in something that they don't believe.

What Happens at Mass?

Erica Brooke Peranski

Saint Gertrude High School, Richmond, Virginia

Mass begins with the gathering rite, which prepares us for the celebration of the Eucharist. The rite includes the priest and other liturgical ministers' processing down an aisle as the assembly sings a hymn. Then everyone in the assembly makes the sign of the cross. The penitential rite for the forgiveness of sins follows. The *Gloria* is then recited or sung, and an opening prayer is offered by the presider.

The first major part of a Catholic Mass is the liturgy of the word. This includes the first reading (usually from the Old Testament), the responsorial psalm (usually led by a cantor with the response sung by the assembly), a second reading (usually from the letters of the New Testament), and a reading from one of the Gospels. The homily follows, wherein the priest explains and connects the Scripture readings to our lives. Then, in unison, we proclaim the Nicene Creed, also known as the Profession of Faith. The general intercessions, which speak to and pray for the needs of the Church and world, conclude the liturgy of the word. This is a very important part of the Mass, because it invites us into a deeper state of worship. It also prepares us for the next part of the Mass, known as the liturgy of the Eucharist.

This part of the Mass includes the preparation of the altar and the presentation of bread and wine. A prayer is said over these gifts, and then the priest begins to pray the Eucharistic prayer on behalf of the community. After a brief opening dialogue, the presider prays the preface, to which the assembly responds, "Holy, holy, holy." The priest then continues the Eucharistic prayer. During the prayer, the wine and bread are consecrated and the community gives thanks to God for all that God has done. Then we pray the Lord's Prayer as a community and exchange the sign of peace with one another.

After this the community says or sings the Lamb of God while the presider breaks the bread. Then we receive Communion, Jesus's Body and Blood, which unites us with God and everyone around us. The Mass ends with the concluding rite, which includes a final blessing, and we are sent forth to love and share the blessings we have just received.

Is the *Lectionary* the Same Thing as a Bible?

Kevin Shaw
Purcell Marian High School, Cincinnati, Ohio

The *Lectionary* is the official book from which the readings selected for the liturgy of the word during Mass are proclaimed. The *Lectionary* is not the Bible, but its content is taken from the Scriptures. The *Lectionary* is based on a special calendar (also called the liturgical cycle) to mark the Church's liturgical celebrations. The liturgical calendar is divided into three years, so over the course of three years, if you attend Mass on a regular basis, you will hear a large portion of the Bible. Year A includes readings from the Gospel of Matthew, year B emphasizes the Gospel of Mark, and year C focuses primarily on the Gospel of Luke. The Gospel of John is included in all three years, especially during Lent and Easter.

In essence the *Lectionary* makes the Bible more accessible to those people who do not commonly read the Scriptures at home.

What's the Difference Between the Regular Year and the Liturgical Year?

Ian Bozant
Notre Dame High School, Sherman Oaks, California

The Church has a special calendar called the liturgical calendar to mark the celebrations of the Church's liturgies.

The Church's liturgical year starts on the first Sunday of Advent. During the subsequent four weeks, we prepare with expectation for the coming of Christ in a spirit of waiting, conversion, and hope.

Following Advent the Church celebrates its second liturgical season. Christmas is upon us, and we celebrate the birth of Christ, our Lord and Savior. The Christmas season lasts from the birth of Christ until his baptism in the Jordan River by Saint John the Baptist (the third Sunday after Christmas).

The next liturgical season is the longest season, and it is split into two parts. It is known as Ordinary Time. This season follows the Baptism of our Lord and lasts until Ash Wednesday. During this time, the Church teaches and meditates on the life, teachings, and miracles of Christ in an effort to lead us more closely to him.

Lent begins on Ash Wednesday, when we recall that we are mere mortals and will return to dust upon death, but through Christ Jesus our souls can be lifted up into everlasting glory. This season is a time of penitence, when we especially recall our sins and make an effort to more closely imitate the life of Christ.

Easter is the season of rejoicing in Christ's victory over sin and death. We celebrate the Easter season from the day of the Resurrection (Easter Sunday—the most important day of the liturgical year) through Pentecost Sunday, when the Apostles received the gifts of the Holy Spirit and began to proclaim the Truth that is Christ.

Following the liturgical season of Easter, the Church resumes the season of Ordinary Time. During this long period, the Church prepares us for the restart of the liturgical cycle, beginning with the first Sunday in Advent.

The liturgical year is important to the Catholic faith because it symbolizes our cycle of life, death, and salvation in Christ.

Why Do We Do the Same Thing at Mass Week After Week?

Kathleen Flynn
Saint Francis Central Coast Catholic High School, Watsonville, California

I have been attending Sunday Mass for seventeen years. That is approximately 884 times, and I can admit that at some point in my seventeen years of life, Mass has been boring. But as I have grown in age and in faith, I have become much more appreciative of the Mass. This means that although I may have heard the "same" readings, made the "same" gestures and responses, and received the "same" Eucharist, none of them are really the same. The experiences, the life that I bring to Mass, are different now than they once were. For example, the story of Jesus's Crucifixion told during Holy Week takes on new meaning and significance now that I've had to deal with my own suffering and pain. Having seen people hungry and in need of food, I have a new perspective of the Eucharist. As my life has grown, so too has my connection with the rituals and practices of the Mass.

One thing we can do so Mass keeps its relevance is to know what is going on and why certain actions are included. This requires some responsibility on our part though. Another thing we can do when we get the feeling that Mass is boring and useless is to talk about it with our parents and teachers. They can give us support and help so we can continue to practice our faith through active participation in the Mass.

We can also remember that there is something wonderful in knowing that people in churches around the world are united each Sunday through the word proclaimed, the prayers recited, and the sacrament received. Through the Eucharist, we become united with Christ and with all other Catholics around the world.

What Is Sacramental Awareness?

Steve Reiss
Saint Pius X High School, Houston, Texas

Sacramental awareness can be described poetically. It is captured well in the opening lines of a poem by Gerard Manley Hopkins: "The world is charged with the grandeur of God."

When we think of sacraments, we can think more broadly than the seven sacraments. A sacrament is something that makes God's hidden presence visible and real to us. The world and everything in it is potentially sacramental in this sense. Because Jesus Christ makes the invisible presence of God known, Catholics refer to Christ as a sacrament. The Church is also considered a sacrament because it makes Christ's presence known. Jesus Christ and the Church and potentially all of creation are sacramental because they communicate and make real to us the presence of God.

Sacramental awareness, or vision, refers to the perspective on the world that is open to seeing God's presence manifested in seemingly ordinary things and events. Catholics believe that the presence of God is all around us and within us. There is not a place in the world where God does not want to be. The challenge for us is to become aware of God's presence and desire to be with us. This is where the seven sacraments come into play. They are special encounters with God.

All the sacraments use symbols that seem rather ordinary—water, oil, bread and wine, and so on. Yet in and through these supposedly ordinary things, we experience the presence of God. In fact, through the power of the Holy Spirit, not only are they transformed, but so are we.

The sacramental rituals that we participate in may only last a short while, but the awareness they invite us to is always before us. The sacraments can be seen as doors that are opened in order to allow us a fuller understanding of God's will.

Are Some Sacraments More Important Than Others?

Andrea Enright
Gibault Catholic High School, Waterloo, Illinois

Each of the seven sacraments plays an important role throughout our lives, but the importance of the seven sacraments relates greatly to the time of life when we are in need of them and receive them.

Beginning at our birth, or shortly thereafter, the first sacrament we receive is the sacrament of Baptism. Just like our physical entrance into this world, Baptism serves as the doorway to our lives as Christians.

As time progresses, we are ready to receive the Lord in other ways—the sacraments of Penance and Reconciliation, Holy Communion, and Confirmation.

Penance and Reconciliation is a sacrament for forgiveness and grace. It frees us from our sins and is a gift from God, conveying grace to our souls.

Holy Communion contributes to our salvation. The Lord's Body and Blood help us resist temptation and avoid sin. Given our frequent reception of Holy Communion weekly during Mass, we recognize the important role the Eucharist plays in our lives. The sacrament of the Eucharist is the "source and summit of the Church" (*Catechism of the Catholic Church*, number 1407).

Confirmation celebrates a person's full and complete membership in the Church.

When we mature, fall in love, and decide to marry, we receive the sacrament of Holy Matrimony. At this time in our lives, we are being united with another as one in the eyes of God. Some people have a different vocation in life; they are called to receive the sacrament of Holy Orders. Those who receive this sacrament are men who are ordained as priests and then dedicate their lives to serving God and God's people.

The last sacrament many of us think of is the Anointing of the Sick. This sacrament is performed when we are approaching the end of our lives or experiencing a serious illness.

Whatever sacrament we may be receiving, we know they all help us grow in our relationship with God.

Why Do Catholics Confess Their Sins to a Priest?

P. J. Thompson
Rockhurst High School, Kansas City, Missouri

Because Jesus was true God and true man, he forgave sins during his earthly ministry. At the end of his earthly ministry, he shared that responsibility with the Apostles. In John 20:21, Jesus said: "Peace be with you. As the Father has sent me, so I send you." Then he breathed on the Apostles and told them: "Receive the Holy Spirit. If you forgive the sins of any, they are forgiven them; if you retain the sins of any, they are retained" (John 20:22–23). Jesus said this because he wanted his Apostles to share in the authority to forgive sins. As the successors to the Apostles, bishops continue to have this power to forgive sins, and they share it with priests. So when we go to confession, we are really going straight to God. We are asking God to forgive our sins, not for a priest to do so.

God gave the Church the authority to forgive sins for a reason. God wanted everyone to share in the power of forgiveness. That is why God includes his disciples in the forgiveness of our sins, and that is why confession to God through a priest is one of the blessed holy sacraments.

What Should I Do If I Don't Believe I'm Ready to Be Confirmed?

Myra Battle
Santa Fe Catholic High School, Lakeland, Florida

Some people may feel that they're not old or mature enough, or that they're not spiritually ready to receive the sacrament of Confirmation. It's okay to not want to be confirmed if you don't feel ready.

Even I had second thoughts about Confirmation. I knew that in this sacrament, I was telling myself and others I wanted to be fully initiated into the Church. For a while, I didn't think I was ready though.

If you have doubts, you might consider talking to a trusted adult, like a parent, a priest, or your Confirmation sponsor. He or she can give you the guidance you need to make the right choice. Perhaps what you thought was an obstacle to celebrating the sacrament can be worked through with prayer, study, and conversation. It is necessary to think things through before making such an important decision. Let the choice be yours, not someone else's. You can listen to the opinions of others, but make up your own mind.

If you decide not to receive the sacrament, your decision should be respected. That being said, just because you decide not to get confirmed now doesn't mean you can't get confirmed later. When you're ready, the Church is waiting.

Why Do People Who Disagree with Church Teaching on Ordination Stay in the Church?

Carolyn Olson
University of Wisconsin-La Crosse, La Crosse, Wisconsin

I never put much thought into the lack of women in leadership positions in the Church until about the time I was ready to be confirmed. I started questioning my pastor about why women could not be priests, but I never got an answer that satisfied me. There were times I even felt more comfortable talking to the women in my church about my faith than I did with my own priest. I often sat in church and analyzed my priest's homilies; I thought I could easily do the same thing, maybe even better.

All these things troubled me. I struggled to understand why women never held the priestly leadership position even though it seemed they were the glue of the Church. Religious education teachers, secretaries, committee organizers, Eucharistic ministers, ushers, cooks, fund-raisers, childcare providers, and custodians were all roles I witnessed women of my Church performing. In my church, it seemed women ran many of the functions and events, but again I never saw a woman leading as a priest.

My dissatisfaction with the Catholic Church and the role of women leaders in the Church has made being proud of my faith difficult. I have thought about leaving the Catholic faith many times, and I struggle daily with my decision to stay with the Church. Many of my friends question why I am still Catholic if I feel so strongly against certain issues in the Church. I made a decision to be confirmed in the Catholic faith, and, in this decision, I also chose to make the Catholic faith my own. I struggle with the Church's current stance on women's ordination, but I choose to be a link in the chain of women's ordination because it is a truth, I feel, the Church will come to recognize over time.

I must admit, however, that this stands in tension with what Pope John Paul II and now Benedict XVI have said about the Church's having no authority to ordain women and that this issue should no longer be discussed. The Church, in this regard, they say, is only following the example of Jesus, who didn't ordain women.

If You Receive the Sacrament of the Anointing of the Sick, Does That Mean You Are Going to Die?

Alex Stewart
Lancaster Catholic High School, Lancaster, Pennsylvania

Receiving the sacrament of the Anointing of the Sick doesn't mean you are going to die. In fact, the *Catechism of the Catholic Church* says: "The anointing of the sick is not a sacrament for those only who are at the point of death. Hence, as soon as anyone of the faithful begins to be in danger of death from sickness or old age, the fitting time for him to receive this sacrament has certainly already arrived"[1] (number 1514).

Some might think that Anointing of the Sick means a person is going to die, because this sacrament is part of what Catholics sometimes refer to as last rites, which are administered to the dying. These rites include Penance and Reconciliation, viaticum (a final reception of Communion, or literally, "food for the journey"), and Anointing of the Sick, but this is not the only time the sacrament is celebrated.

In the sacrament of the Anointing of the Sick, a priest lays hands on the head of the sick person and anoints her or him with blessed oil. The person is then prayed over by all present. It is then both a personal and communal experience. Through it the person meets Jesus the healer.

As for the people who receive this sacrament, they are, as might be expected, the suffering and the ill. My mother, a few years back, received this sacrament before she went to Johns Hopkins University Hospital to be evaluated for a brain tumor. Anointing of the sick was used to protect my mother in the face of anything unexpected and to comfort my family. It certainly didn't mean she was going to die.

I'm Considering a Religious Vocation. What Should I Do to See Whether This Is Really My Calling?

Margaret R. Durham
Saint Pius X High School, Houston, Texas

The consideration of a religious vocation—a life of service to Christ and the Church as a priest, brother, or sister—is a very important process. One way to explore a religious vocation is to examine it by discussing options with an adult who has chosen a life of religious vocation.

In this process of discernment, a person might ask himself or herself if he or she is willing to do the spiritual work associated with the path to religious life, and if he or she has an active prayer life, a strong relationship with God. Daily prayer and communication with God is the foundation of such a life. A person choosing a religious vocation must be willing to accept the responsibility of necessary religious vows truthfully and wholly (poverty, chastity, and obedience).

In a sexually charged culture, religious vocations present the challenge of the vow of celibacy. Though life in a religious vocation is not lonely, it lacks the support and partnership of marriage. Yet celibacy also can free a person to see beyond her or his family in service to the Church and world.

Additionally, the idea of making some sacrifices to serve God and the Church can seem frightening or difficult (the vow of obedience, for example).

A person considering a religious vocation must also ask if he or she can live a life of simplicity. Taking a vow of poverty ensures that a person will use only what is necessary rather than living in excess.

The final question a person might ask herself or himself is this: Is my life an example of faith in action and service to God?

Why Is It Necessary for Catholics to Get Married in the Church?

Charles Andrew Janssen
Saint Thomas High School, Houston, Texas

Getting married today can seem like entering a three-ring circus. Once you find the love of your life, you have to ask if he or she will marry you, usually in some fantastic way like fireworks that spell out "Marry Me!" when they explode. Elaborate planning follows for the wedding of your dreams. The focus here is often on the party afterward instead of on the ceremony. Then you go to a judge, a cruise-ship captain, an Elvis impersonator, or some other licensed person to perform the task of marrying you and your partner. After that—good luck!

The Catholic Church provides another alternative. Most Catholic churches advise couples wanting to get married to announce their intention six months (or more) in advance. In addition to the practical planning of securing a church, getting a caterer, and deciding on the honeymoon spot, there is spiritual planning to do. According to the Church, marriage is a sacred commitment for life. The phrase "until death do us part" is taken seriously (*The Rites*, page 715). Couples usually meet with their pastor (and sometimes others) a number of times to discuss what marriage is all about—commitment, fidelity, unity between spouses, and openness to new life. One of the key ideas the Church points out is that marriage is not an event (the wedding), but it is a process (the lifelong commitment of husband and wife).

The Church requires that weddings take place in a church before witnesses that represent the Christian community. Having a wedding in a church establishes its religious dimension. By getting married in the Church, the couple publicly admits that God plays an important role in their lives and will provide necessary support to sustain their relationship. The couple wants and needs God's blessing for this important step in life. The couple also needs the support of their families and friends. This is why weddings are public ceremonies, not private ones.

Finally, in and through one's own marriage or the witnessing of another's, one catches a glimpse of the love of God made manifest.

5 Teens Share Their Understanding of Prayer and Spirituality

Does God Always Answer Our Prayers?

Laura Ashley Nuestro
John Paul II High School, Hendersonville, Tennessee

God does answers all prayers, but sometimes the answer is "no," sometimes it is "not yet," and other times it is "yes." We don't really know why God answers different prayers in different ways except that God, being all-wise and all-knowing, is aware of what is best for us, and sometimes that is to answer a prayer in the negative.

Think of a small child who wants ice cream just before his dinner. If his parents are wise, they will say no because they know that granting this request at that time is inappropriate. God is also a wise parent, and many times our prayer requests are not in our best interest, regardless of what we may think.

When we pray, God may not answer all our prayers the way we had hoped, but in the process, we may discover that what we originally prayed for wasn't what we needed in the first place.

Why Should I Pray? What Purpose Does It Serve?

Mackenzie Staron
Santa Fe Catholic High School, Lakeland, Florida

If we want a relationship with God, we can't live without prayer. If there's no communication, there's no connection. Prayer is how we communicate with God. Prayer is a form of serving God (see Luke 2:36–38). We pray because God commands us to pray (see Philippians 4:6–7).

Prayer can help us grow in our relationship with God. When we pray, we don't have to say a formal prayer; we can talk directly to God like we are having a conversation with a good friend. In some ways, it's not *how* we come to God, just that we've come. Prayer is like opening a door to let God in. Prayer can also heal us and help us become more loving in our relationships with others.

In situations for which we do not know specifically what God's will is, prayer is a means of discerning God's will. In one sense, prayer is like sharing the Gospel with people. We do not know who will respond to the message of the Gospel until we share it. It is the same with prayer: We will never see the results of answered prayer until we pray.

We pray to demonstrate our faith in God. When we pray, we are telling God that we love God.

Are There Different Types of Prayer?

Kristin Allene McNamara
Saint Francis Central Coast Catholic High School, Watsonville, California

Often when people think of prayer, they think of Mass or of a person kneeling, head bowed, and saying a silent prayer, but this is not the only type of prayer. Prayer can be personal or communal; silent, spoken, or sung; formal or informal. It can even be as simple as taking a minute out of the day to stop and give thanks.

Not all prayer is structured or has a format. However, the Catholic Church recognizes four types of prayer: adoration (praising God), contrition (asking God's forgiveness), thanksgiving (thanking God), and supplication (humbly asking God for something).

Everything that increases our awareness of God is prayer. Whether we are praying the Psalms, the Lord's Prayer, the Scriptures, personal and intercessory prayers, or our favorite hymn, we are in prayer. Prayer can even be done through actions. It is said that actions speak louder than words. If everybody acted in a prayerful manner by loving their neighbors or by leading faithful lives, the world would be in perfect harmony. There really is no "correct" way to pray, nor is there an incorrect way. Yes, it should be reverent, but it's okay to be angry or upset while praying. Praying can be a way to vent emotions and to give up all our sufferings to the Lord.

How Is Music an Expression of Prayer?

Monica MacLean
Saint Francis Catholic High School, Gainesville, Florida

Throughout history and up to the present, people have expressed their praise, disapproval, feelings, and love through song. This is especially true in our worship of God. Song is like a form of light that God pushes through the body of a singer. As a singer at church, I feel that all people can express their love for, and devotion to, God through singing. That's why it's important that everyone sing, not just those with the best voices.

The heavenly angels of the Lord have been thought for ages to sing and praise God with all their beautiful voices. Many people in the Bible praised God too, like Moses after he delivered God's Chosen People out of the pharaoh's slavery (see Exodus, chapter 15). As stated in the Hebrew Scriptures, during large gatherings of people, celebrations were conducted to praise God with song, music, and dance.

The Psalms in the Bible have stated that singing is a traditional way to praise God. "Sing to him a new song; / play skillfully on the strings, with loud shouts" (Psalm 33:3). Singing is a way to open up to God and God's grace. Music can be considered an instrumental part of our praise of, and prayer to, God.

How Do Postures—Standing, Sitting, Kneeling, and Bowing—Help Us with Prayer?

Vianey Colli
Bishop Lynch High School, Dallas, Texas

It is important to know that God is always listening to our prayers, whether we are standing, sitting, kneeling, or bowing. In some cases, people with physical disabilities are not able to stand, sit, kneel, or bow, so they pray in a way that they are able to, and God listens.

The same way our faces can express emotions when we're sad, happy, or angry, our bodies also have a language. Our body language should express to God that God is the one we worship and respect and that we want God to listen and help us in our prayer. For example, if someone prefers to stand while praying, he or she should make sure to stand up straight and not let his or her body language express something he or she doesn't want it to express.

So, when it comes to praying to God, we must choose a posture that makes us comfortable and focused, but, no matter what, we must know God is always by our side listening to us.

Could You Offer Me Any Prayer Guidelines?

Katherine T. Schilling
Saint Teresa's Academy, Kansas City, Missouri

Prayer is anything we do that deepens or strengthens our relationship with God. So anyone can pray anytime, anywhere, and for any reason. Prayer can be a formal recitation of a traditional prayer, a personal conversation with God, or even the way we live our lives.

Prayer can be expressed with others or alone, and in song, speech, silence, or action. We can pray by performing a piano piece or playing a basketball game. We can pray by dancing or painting. We can pray by taking a walk or working hard at soccer practice. We can pray by helping around the house or doing homework. There are no rules when it comes to praying. Pray in the shower! Pray when you are getting dressed, making your bed, brushing your teeth, combing your hair, going to school, preparing for a test, switching classes, eating a snack, taking out the trash, unloading the dishwasher, or heading to work. Pray when you are stopped at a red light in the car or waiting in line at the grocery store.

Still, in the midst of a busy world, it is important for us to remember to consciously seek a quiet place and time to just be with God. Whether these peaceful moments are outside on a sunny afternoon, or in our room before we go to bed, they allow us to strengthen our relationship with God.

How Did Jesus **Pray?**

Katie Werle
Cotter High School, Winona, Minnesota

The Gospels tell us that Jesus prayed for and about nearly everything in his life, from strength, guidance, and comfort to safekeeping and protection. Jesus kept an attitude of complete dependency on, and constant communication with, God. Perhaps his greatest teaching on prayer is found in the Lord's Prayer (see Luke 11:2–4).

The Scriptures tell us that there were times when Jesus prayed early in the morning (see Mark 1:35), all through the night (see Luke 6:12), and many times when he went to pray by himself on a mountain or in a garden or desert (see Mathew 14:23, 26:36, 4:1).

These patterns are also how Jesus wanted us to pray, so he told his followers:

And whenever you pray, do not be like the hypocrites; for they love to stand and pray in the synagogues and at the street corners, so that they may be seen by others. Truly I tell you, they have received their reward. But whenever you pray, go into your room and shut the door and pray to your Father who is in secret; and your Father who sees in secret will reward you. (Matthew 6:5–6)

Forgiveness and an ultimate faith in God were apparent in the prayers of Jesus. In the Garden of Gethsemane, Jesus said, "Father, if you are willing, remove this cup from me; yet not my will but yours be done" (Luke 22:42).

The last key that is essential to understanding more about Jesus's prayer, life, and death is what he said while dying on the cross. He said, "Father, forgive them; for they do not know what they are doing" (Luke 23:34). Jesus was full of forgiveness and compassion, even for those who were going to kill him, because he knew that ultimately his Father knew what was best.

Is It Okay to Pray for Myself?

Meredith R. Mulcahy
Saint Francis Xavier Church, Winthrop, Maine

As we get older, we should make a conscious effort to pray for others. Yet no matter what we pray for, from world peace to a snow day, in the end, it is perfectly fine to pray for ourselves as well. Praying for ourselves is not selfish; it simply means we recognize we need God's love, guidance, and care to live out each day in the best way possible. The important thing to remember is to thank God for everything God does for us and gives to us.

Because prayer is about working on our relationship with God, it makes sense to share with God our deepest worries, our greatest joys, and our requests to become better, holier people. Prayer is not, however, about getting what we want. Saying to God, "I need your help," or "Please watch over me" is an excellent way of acknowledging our need for God's presence, each moment of our lives.

What Is the Value of Praying to Saints When We Can Go Directly to God?

William P. Johnson
Xavier High School, New York, New York

A saint is someone who devoted her or his life to serving God and others and is now in heaven with God. When we pray to a saint, we ask that saint to present our prayer and intention to God, to plead our petition before the Lord. We do such a thing because people who love one another hold one another up before God in prayer. Just because a person has died doesn't mean she or he no longer needs our prayers or cannot bring our needs before God in heaven.

In the Scriptures, Jesus says we should pray always and with much enthusiasm when we pray for a petition that is extremely important: "Ask, and it will be given you; search, and you will find; knock, and the door will be opened for you" (Matthew 7:7).

Now if we have someone else who would pray to God along with us, say a saint, why wouldn't we use that resource? The Catholic Tradition calls this the communion of saints: the belief that we are in union with not only the living but also the dead. All those who have left us in faith are not gone—grandparents, aunts and uncles, and family friends—but are advocating for us, supporting us in faith, before God. Though Jesus is the one true mediator, it never hurts to get a little help from family and friends.

Why Do Catholics Fast During Lent?

Christopher Rivera

Loyola High School, Los Angeles, California

Lent is the season of the Church year when we prepare for the mysteries of Easter: Christ's death and Resurrection. This period lasts forty days, paralleling the forty days and nights Jesus spent in the desert.

During his time in the desert, Jesus was constantly being tempted by Satan. Jesus was there to strengthen his faith and prepare for his public ministry.

To experience this same challenge and achieve a spiritual state such as Jesus did, it is customary that Catholics fast during Lent. Especially during the Lenten season, we seek to strengthen our faith and show our gratitude for the ultimate deed Jesus fulfilled to save us from sin.

The Church requires that during the season of Lent, we abstain from meat on Ash Wednesday as well as each Friday of Lent and Good Friday.

Although most will abstain from meat on Fridays, others will choose to fast the entire day so they can at least sample the hardship Jesus suffered during those excruciating forty days and nights in the desert.

Another practice Catholics engage in is the sacrificing of something during the forty days of Lent. During this time, many people choose to give up something small such as a favorite snack, drink, or routine trips to the movies, mall, or arcade. Others choose to make a commitment to God that they will pray more, work on being kinder to others, or change their attitude.

The true purpose of Lent and these rituals is to help Catholics strengthen their faith while preparing for the death and Resurrection of Jesus.

Why Are Catholics So Devoted to the Rosary?

Patrick Sardo Pirozzi
Delbarton School, Morristown, New Jersey

We meditate on the mysteries to place ourselves in the presence of Christ and his mother, Mary. The rosary is a progression of prayers, including the Apostles' Creed, the Lord's Prayer, the Hail Mary, and the Glory Be. These prayers are grouped into different devotions, called mysteries. The Church recognizes four types of mysteries: the joyful mysteries, the luminous mysteries (added by Pope John Paul II), the sorrowful mysteries, and the glorious mysteries.

By praying the rosary, we try to put ourselves in union with the moments in the lives of Christ and his mother and reflect on how these apply to our own lives.

The rosary is a prayer offered to the Blessed Mother. As the mother of God, Mary is our mother, and we pray to her in her honor. In being Christ's mother, Mary takes on a maternal role for all humans, as we are all the children of God. The rosary is a request raised to Mary with the belief that she will bring these prayers to her Son, Jesus.

What Is the Ignatian Examen of Conscience?

Charles James LeSueur
Brophy College Preparatory, Phoenix, Arizona

Not only is the daily examination of conscience a foundational characteristic of the Society of Jesus (more commonly known as the Jesuits), but it is also an important part of the spiritual life of many Catholics. The practice of the examination originated in the *Spiritual Exercises,* by Saint Ignatius of Loyola, a former soldier who became the founder of the Jesuits.

The examen contains five successive points of self-discipline. In the first point, we thank God for the blessings received in our lives; in the second, we ask for the grace to recognize our flaws (we often want to hide them); in the third, we review the passing of the day, noting what failures we committed in deed or thought; in the fourth, we ask God's pardon; and in the fifth, we resolve to amend for our actions.

My own high school partakes in the examination of conscience daily after our lunch period. As a time of meditation and reflection, I look over my actions throughout the day to see if they have been parallel to whom I actually want to become. Then I seek to discover the grace of God within my own life.

I believe that this second part is vital. Attending Catholic schools my entire life, I have found it unsettlingly easy to come to see God as a distant figure limited to the inside covers of bibles or within the walls of religion class and not an integral presence in my life.

The examen provides a time of self-reflection that sweeps aside the veils that can blind people from the presence of God in their everyday actions, intentions, and words.

What Is *Lectio Divina?*

Lauren A. Puryear
Mary Help of Christians High School, North Haledon, New Jersey

The *lectio divina* (divine reading) is a quiet, meditative way of reading a Scripture passage and listening to what the Holy Spirit is telling us through it. *Lectio* can be done in a group or individually.

The process of *lectio* is really quite simple. It is divided into five steps with Latin names: *lectio, meditatio, oratio, contemplatio,* and *actio.* In *lectio* the leader reads a chosen Scripture passage aloud. During the reading, the participants listen attentively and prayerfully to hear the voice of God. Then there is a time of silence to meditate (meditatio) on the part of the Scripture passage that stands out the most (this might be a simple word or phrase). This first step can be repeated up to three times. Then there is an extended period for the participants to talk with God (oratio), to reflect on the meaning of the passage, and to write down the part of Scripture passage that the Holy Spirit places on their hearts.

While reflecting on that certain Scripture passage, the participants might ask themselves questions such as, "How does this pertain to my life?" or "What is God trying to show me through this Scripture passage?" After all the participants have completed this step, they can then voluntarily share what the Holy Spirit told them. This time is also devoted to responding to God in some form of personal prayer. This often is followed by *contemplatio,* a period of "resting in the Lord." Here the participants simply sit in the presence of God.

Actio is not an actual step in the prayer, but it is a reminder to the participants that their time with God's word will have an effect on the way they live.

Lectio divina can be prayed on a regular basis, because it helps people get closer to God and understand the messages God conveys through the Scriptures and the Holy Spirit. The purpose of *lectio divina* is to keep people in tune with God and the Holy Spirit; it also enhances their spiritual and prayer life.

Why Do Some Catholics Go on Pilgrimages?

Alyssa Perrella and Catherine A. Piasio
Villa Walsh Academy, Morristown, New Jersey

Pilgrimages have a significant meaning. They are a time to take a break from worldly things, a time of reflection and renewal. Pilgrims are privileged enough to visit sacred shines and the holy places of our ancestors. A pilgrimage is not a vacation; it is time to refocus our relationship with Christ. A pilgrimage is a personal invitation from God. It is a journey to a holy, sacred place.

This past summer, I was privileged to attend World Youth Day in Cologne, Germany. Three things really impressed me about this pilgrimage experience: (1) meeting people of the same faith, (2) witnessing how personable Pope Benedict XVI is, and (3) seeing the number of people who were present. We met people from Italy, France, Syria, Germany, Argentina, England, Portugal, Australia, Ireland, and the United States. Though a challenge, it was fun to talk to them and try to understand their languages and strong accents. Not only did I meet people from other countries, but I met Americans from different states and towns.

There were over one million young people at this wonderful event, and it didn't matter what country we came from, what language we spoke, or what age we were. We were all there to proclaim the same faith, to praise Jesus, and to grow closer to God.

What Are the Stations of the Cross, and Why Do Catholics Pray Them?

Julia Clancy
Saint Pius X High School, Houston, Texas

Early Christians often recounted the story of Jesus's Passion, death, and Resurrection by making pilgrimages to Jerusalem, eager to walk the way of Jesus's last hours. Those who were unable to make the pilgrimage to Jerusalem began to create models of the journey, known as stations, in their communities and churches.

The stations of the cross is a way for Catholics to visualize the suffering and death of Jesus. A person meditates on each station, imagining being there at Calvary (or Golgotha). The stations are present in most Catholic churches.

The stations of the cross is not an exact historical retelling of Jesus's journey to the cross; in fact, many of the stations (numbers 3,

4, 6, 7, and 9) have no basis in the Scriptures at all. However, in 1991 Pope John Paul II created a new way of praying the way of the cross: fourteen stations all based on the Scriptures.

Although the stations are prayed more often during Lent, many people meditate on them year round. The stations are synonymous with Lent, Holy Week, and Good Friday.

There are fourteen stations. The traditional stations are as follows: (1) Jesus is condemned to death, (2) Jesus takes up his cross, (3) Jesus falls the first time, (4) Jesus meets his mother, (5) Simon helps Jesus carry the cross, (6) Veronica wipes the face of Jesus, (7) Jesus falls the second time, (8) Jesus meets the women of Jerusalem, (9) Jesus falls the third time, (10) Jesus is stripped of his garments, (11) Jesus is nailed to the cross, (12) Jesus dies on the cross, (13) Jesus is taken down from the cross, and (14) Jesus is laid in the tomb.

In certain variations of the stations, a fifteenth station is added to represent Jesus's rising from the dead. The stations were created so people could come to know the last days of Jesus.

Can I Use Words Like *Friend, Brother,* or *Coach* When Praying to God?

Megan Deye
Ursuline Academy, Cincinnati, Ohio

God is the Almighty Father, our Creator, our King, the Holy One—the list continues. For some theses titles may portray God as a far-off, somewhat mysterious being to whom we should pray and give praise. Yet the Church tells us there are many possible titles for God.

Sure, Shepherd and Savior tell us God will guide us and save us, but during the rough times in our lives, we may need a specific image of God with a more personal connection than these vague, far-off words. We need to understand *how* God will guide us and what God expects from us in return. For example, if we just need someone to talk to, we can pray to God as our friend. This image lets us know God will listen to us, reassure us, and walk beside us, like a good friend often does.

If we are facing a difficulty, we can pray to God as a sort of coach. As a coach, God will give us the tools, support, and guidance we need to get through the tough times, just like a good coach would do.

When Jesus taught his disciples about God, he described God in his disciples' terms. He knew they understood the relationship a shepherd has with his sheep, so he described God as a shepherd. In the same way, it is up to us to learn what Jesus taught about God and to apply it to our lives in a way that allows us to grow in our relationship with God.

6 Teens Share Their Understanding of Mary and the Saints

How Does a Person Become a Saint?

Brittany Bartucci
Saint Rose High School, Belmar, New Jersey

"Santo subito"—*Make him a saint now.* I heard these words chanted by the crowds gathered outside Saint Peter's for the funeral of Pope John Paul II. As important as he was, and as holy a life he led, there is more to being declared a saint than public acclamation.

In a special way, the Church encourages all of us to holiness by raising up as examples women and men who have lived especially holy lives. The Catholic Church calls them saints. The process by which someone becomes a saint is called canonization. According to the Catholic Church, the Pope does not make someone a saint; rather, the designation of sainthood only recognizes what God has already done.

For centuries saints were chosen through public opinion. However, in the tenth century, Pope John XV developed an official canonization process. The process of becoming a Catholic saint is very lengthy, often taking decades or centuries to complete.

To begin the process, at least five years need to have passed since the person's death (in special cases this can be waived). A group of people from a diocese or parish—often called the promoter group—goes to the bishop of the diocese, who begins the investigation. The bishop investigates the candidate's life and writings for evidence of heroic virtue and interviews people who knew the person. The bishop then sends a report to Rome. A summary called the *positio* is presented to the Congregation for the Causes of Saints, the Vatican body that oversees the canonization process. From there the would-be saint's cause is in the hands of the Vatican.

It's the job of the Congregation for the Causes of Saints to determine whether this person led a life of heroic virtue. If so, the person is then proclaimed by the Pope as venerable. Unless the person is a martyr (died for the faith), a miracle is needed to move to the next stage—beatification. Here the Church declares that this person is in heaven and may intercede on our behalf. In order for a person to be beatified, he or she must be shown as responsible for a posthumous (after earthly life) miracle.

For canonization into sainthood, another miracle is needed. This miracle needs to have occurred after the person's beatification. The Pope then declares canonization at a special Mass in the saint's honor. It usually takes place outside in Saint Peter's Square before large crowds, but sometimes it is conducted in the saint's home country. The person is given a feast day, usually the date of death, on which his or her witness of faith is celebrated annually.

What Is the Difference Between All Saints' Day and All Souls' Day?

Katie Anderson
Saint Elizabeth's High School, Wilmington, Delaware

All Saints' Day and All Souls' Day happen around one of my favorite times of year—Halloween. These two days remind us that in the midst of trick-or-treating, the Church is celebrating the sacred witness of its saints and departed faithful.

All Saints' Day, celebrated on November 1, honors all known and unknown Christian saints and martyrs who have served as models of faith to the Church. All Saints' Day was originally celebrated on the first Sunday after Pentecost but was changed to November 1 by Pope Gregory III. On that date, he consecrated a chapel in Saint Peter's Basilica to all saints and martyrs. The chapel serves as a resting place for many of their relics. In 835, at the insistence of Pope Gregory IV, All Saints' Day was later decreed a holy day of obligation, meaning that all Catholics must attend Mass on the day.

All Souls' Day, on the other hand, commemorates the souls of those who have died but have not yet entered into heaven. These souls still need to be cleansed from the venial sins committed during life and can be aided through our prayer. The celebration of All Souls' Day also serves as a reminder to Catholics of the need to live an upright and moral life. This feast is celebrated on November 2. Unlike All Saints' Day, All Souls' Day is not a holy day of obligation. However, special Masses are offered throughout the day for the benefit of those souls in Purgatory.

A celebration that takes place during these two days is known as *Dia de Los Muertos,* or the Day of the Dead. This celebration has become more visible in recent years due to the increasing population of Mexican-Americans. Honoring deceased family members, people visit cemeteries and churches to pray, light candles, and perform other signs of respect.

Were Saints Normal People?

Olivia Mae Waring
Villa Walsh Academy, Morristown, New Jersey

The saints came from different centuries, different countries, and different backgrounds, but they experienced the same emotions as every other person. They were hungry, thirsty, joyful, content, exhausted, angry, despondent, jealous, afraid, and altogether human. What sets them apart from others is not their ability to understand God's will or even to carry it out successfully, but rather their capacity to accept the Creator's word and to try to fulfill whatever task God had prepared for them.

Becoming a saint does not always occur in a single flash of understanding, an instantaneous acquisition of zeal, or a brilliant vision of God; rather, sainthood requires a lifetime of cultivation. It involves moments of lethargy when one would rather not get out of bed to face another day of struggling against sin. It involves moments of despair when one would like nothing better than to crawl back into bed and hide under the covers from persecution and failure. And it involves a few shimmering moments of utter peace.

One cannot say the saints were "normal." They possessed the remarkable gift of being able to trust in God and follow God willingly. Yet so does everyone. Whatever our history or abilities, we are all bound on one inescapable journey toward a greater existence. Sainthood simply depends on recognizing one's potential for faith in God and acting upon it. No, the saints were not normal. But neither am I, neither are you, and neither is anyone who comes from God and is destined to return to God.

Is It Okay to Pray **for Dead Relatives and Friends?**

Candice Norrell
Saint Mary's University of Minnesota, Winona, Minnesota

As Catholics we believe that when you die, you go to Purgatory to be purified before entering into the fullness of God. Emphasizing the communal nature of our faith, we, in faith, are asked to believe and practice that it is a holy and pious thought to pray for the dead, that they may be freed from sins (see 2 Maccabees 12:45–46).

Praying for the dead is one of the greatest spiritual works of mercy. Once they have been loosed from their sins and are in heaven, our deceased relatives and friends have been purified. They, in turn, endlessly pray for us out of gratitude for our aid in their obtaining heaven. It is perfectly okay to pray for them, especially now, for they are in heaven interceding on our behalf.

The Catholic Church has always honored the dead by offering prayers in suffrage for them, and above all, offering the Holy Mass for them, so they may be helped in their purification process. Almsgiving, indulgences, and works of penance undertaken on behalf of the dead are also allowed—even encouraged—in the Church. Saint John Chrysostom said: "Let us help and commemorate [the dead]. If Job's sons were purified by their father's sacrifice, why would we doubt that our offerings for the dead bring them some consolation? Let us not hesitate to help those who have died and to offer our prayers for them"[2] (*Catechism of the Catholic Church*, number 1032).

Though this process can be aided by our actions, God is the one who saves.

Are There Any Teenage Saints?

Rachel Irene Victoria Thompson
Saint Agnes Academy, Houston, Texas

Teenagers today face numerous challenges, many of which originate from sources such as the media, peer pressure, and self-image. Therefore it's essential that today's youth fight sin and model their lives after someone who lived her or his life with love, mercy, and a generous heart: a saint. Although there are many teen saints, like Saint Maria Goretti, Saint Agnes, Saint Sebastian, Saint Mark, and Saint Stanislaus Kostka, there is one saint whose adolescent years parallel the life of a modern teen: Saint Joan of Arc.

Saint Joan of Arc (1412–1431) was a follower of God's grace, will, and love. She heard heavenly voices calling to her and was ridiculed for it. Now it is true that most of us do not see angels, talk to saints, or blatantly hear God's voice. We could instead consider these "voices" not as literal, audible booming sounds calling our name from on high, but rather as a form of conscience. Are we not sometimes ridiculed for listening to that nagging little "voice," our conscience? for doing what is right rather than what is wrong? for saying no to drugs and premarital sex even when others pressure us to do so? That is the Lord's way of speaking to us, calling us to accountability. God is the voice of our conscience.

Saint Joan of Arc lived her life with conviction. She is just one of many who chose to please God rather than those around her. Although she lived in a different time, her life serves as a model for our own. We can pray to Saint Joan of Arc (her feast day is May 30) and to other saints to help us conquer evil and intervene on our behalf that we may live a pure life dedicated to God.

How Can I Be More Like the Saints?

Dan Bossaller
Saint Pius X High School, Houston, Texas

This important question was answered in one sentence by my sixth-grade teacher: Practice random acts of kindness. Go out of your way, she said, to help a person you may not even know. It can be as simple as opening a door for a teacher, saying a kind word to a classmate, or helping a younger sibling with homework.

"The Little Flower," Saint Thérèse of Lisieux (1873–1897), achieved her sainthood and became a doctor of the Church—a person not only of great holiness but also someone who has taught the truths of the faith in an exemplary way by performing random acts of kindness just like those previously mentioned. As a girl of fourteen, she realized she could not do "big things," so she decided to perform small acts of charity. Some years later, she passed away unknown and unrecognized. But not for long. Through her journal, *The Story of a*

Soul, the Catholic Church realized she was someone who did small things that passed under the radar of most people. It was, however, the small things she did with great love to bring glory to God that led to her being declared a saint. People do not like to accept distasteful jobs without complaint. However, you could help a student carry his or her books to class. Something as small as taking time out of your schedule to talk to a teacher or sibling means a whole lot to both the teacher or sibling and God. Expect nothing in return for these acts of kindness, because the reward is greater in heaven—greater than the best earthly reward imaginable!

Saint Thérèse of Lisieux's challenge is to make these acts a daily habit. You will be surprised at how much happier you will feel. Be mindful of your surroundings, because as the Little Flower showed us, the little things make a big difference.

How Can We Relate to Saints When We Live in a Completely Different World and Time?

Scott Collard
Lexington Catholic High School, Lexington, Kentucky

The truth is that human nature never changes. Sin continues to feed problems of greed, segregation, and hate. The challenges saints addressed hundreds of years ago are similar to the problems we face today. To understand this, we must be aware that saints are living among us right now! All people can become saints in God's eyes; official recognition by the Church isn't required. Small acts of kindness can be as moving as giving fortunes to the poor.

Just like then, being a saint today isn't easy! Luckily, the saints were people just like you and me. A lot of times they experienced self-doubt. Also just like us, many saints wanted to have fun. And, just like us, they weren't perfect!

An example is Saint Francis of Assisi. He lived in an influential family, whose father wanted him to take up the family business and make a name for himself. He grew up in comfort, spent a lot of time partying, and did not care about his grades. Like many people our age, he may have thought (however wrongly!) that religion was confining. During his early adulthood, Francis began to hear a call from God. It took a lot of prayer and sometimes doing things wrong for Francis to get to know God and God's mission, and even then Francis made mistakes. He was sometimes overly judgmental, but he worked hard to show others the love he felt. His spirit was infectious.

Just like Francis, we aren't perfect people, but we should strive to serve God. We can discover what God is calling us to do in this world by getting to know God and by leading saintly lives with God as our guide. This doesn't necessarily require rebuilding churches or giving up everything to live in the desert. But it does require that we love our enemies, treat everyone with respect, and open our eyes to God. That concept will not change in anyone's lifetime.

What Makes Mary Different from the Other Saints?

Lauren
Gibault Catholic High School, Waterloo, Illinois

Mary had a close relationship with her Son, Jesus. She witnessed Jesus's life and death. She would later attest to his Resurrection. Mary's life was full of faithfulness and love; she believed, trusted, and lived by God's word. In this sense, she can be called the first disciple.

Born free from the original sin that affects human beings, Mary was selected by God with special reasoning. Her response to God's invitation of discipleship through her motherhood of Jesus is the response of all those who aspire to be like the saints: "Let it be with me according to your word" (Luke 1:38).

Many of the saints showed a strong love and dedication to the Lord, but Mary had a direct tie with the Lord that only she could share with her Son. As Catholics we pray in thanksgiving for her witness. We also ask her to pray for us, knowing that it will lead to her Son, Jesus.

Just What Exactly Is the Immaculate Conception?

Sarah Pottratz
Brebeuf Jesuit Preparatory School, Indianapolis, Indiana

Many people are under the impression that the Immaculate Conception is the miracle that allowed God to become human in the womb of Mary, but in actuality, the Immaculate Conception is the religious truth that Mary was conceived without original sin. This means that unlike the rest of us, Mary was born with an absolute openness to God and God's will in her life.

According to the Catholic faith, God wanted someone sinless to be the mother of God's Son, so God chose Mary to be conceived without any blemishes from the sin of Adam and Eve. This teaching is revealed to us in the Scriptures. We can turn to Luke 1:28 where the Archangel Gabriel appears to Mary in Nazareth and says: "Greetings, favored one! The Lord is with you." This greeting tells us Mary was in special grace with God.

A central tenet of the Immaculate Conception is that Mary still had free will. Although she was not born with original sin and she did not have quite the same tendencies we have inherited because of our blemished souls, Mary could still be tempted and still had to say yes to God. However, this is all the more reason to love Mary and try to model our lives after her. She is the perfect servant of God whom we should all strive to be more like.

Who Is **Our Lady of Guadalupe?**

P. Grant Janssen

Saint Thomas High School, Houston, Texas

After the Spanish conquest of Mexico in 1521, the native population, the Aztecs, were not accepting of Christianity. This is understandable given the way many of them were treated by Spanish colonialists. The archbishop of Mexico City, however, routinely prayed for a way to increase conversions and the success of missionaries. His plea was finally answered in 1531, when Mary, in the appearance of an Aztec princess, appeared to a poor Native American worker named Juan Diego.

Mary requested that Juan visit the archbishop and ask him to build a church on Tepeyac Hill (near present-day Mexico City). Juan Diego visited the skeptical bishop several times. Juan Diego returned to Mary and asked for some kind of proof to convince the bishop. She told Juan to gather some roses at the top of a hill, put them in his cloak (also called *tilma*), and then bring them to the bishop as proof. He did as he was told and dropped the roses at the bishop's feet. Because roses did not grow at that time of year and in that place, when they hit the floor, the bishop and all other witnesses fell to their knees and prayed. Additionally, an image of Our Lady of Guadalupe that no human hand could have made appeared on the cloak.

The Aztecs came to believe that this miracle showed that God loved and accepted them because Mary appeared not to a European, but to one of their own people. One can still see the cloak of Juan Diego today. It hangs in the Basilica of Our Lady of Guadalupe in Mexico City. Today the descendants of the Aztecs are often considered some of the most devout Catholics in the world.

As the Church in America continues to be influenced by Hispanic Catholics, Our Lady of Guadalupe will likely become more widely known.

How Can Mary Appear to People When She's Already in Heaven?

Jessica Kerwin
Ursuline Academy, Springfield, Illinois

Picture it: Due to a steady rain, you're standing on muddy ground and your clothes are soaked. For the past few months, you've heard stories of the Virgin Mary appearing to three young children in your little village of Fátima. Today is the day (doubted by many) that Mary promised she would prove the authenticity of what the small children were saying. As you stare at the sky, along with fifty to seventy thousand other people, it seems as if the sun has come alive. It moves closer and closer to the earth and dances, and numerous colors fill the sky. Wonder and fear fill those around you. You kneel down and pray as the sun continues to rapidly dive toward the earth, swelling in magnitude. Then, suddenly, the sun stops in its place, suspended in the air, until it finally takes its normal position in the sky again. Miraculously, both the ground and your clothes are dry.

This is an example of one of the most famous Marian apparitions known to the world today. It happened in Fátima, Portugal, on October 13, 1917. As the name suggests, a Marian apparition is an occurrence of Mary appearing. Some of the most famous sightings of these apparitions have been at Fátima, Guadalupe, Lourdes, and though not officially recognized by the Church, Medjugorje.

The appearances of Mary are examples of private revelation. Unlike public revelation, which includes teachings of the Scriptures and Tradition, Catholics are not required to believe in private revelation. Regardless, most Catholics recognize and accept the importance of these revelations as long as they agree with Church teachings.

It cannot be scientifically explained how Mary appears when she's already dead. However, as Christians, we know Mary comes because God willed her to. So why would God want her to appear to us—for the same reason God sent Christ—to teach us how much God loves us and how much God wants to forgive us our sins. Because Mary is the mother of God, we can look to her as a way of getting closer to her Son. We too learn to look to Mary as a way to love Christ more.

How Can We Explain to Those Who Are Not Catholic That We Admire and Respect Mary but Do Not Worship Her?

Sarah Berlinger

Trenton Catholic Academy, Hamilton, New Jersey

"Hail Mary, full of grace." These are the first few words of one of the most scriptural, traditional, popular and recited prayers in Catholicism. To many, Mary, the mother of Jesus, is an image of hope, courage, determination, and love. We pray to Mary and ask her to intercede on our behalf. To those who are not Catholic, it may seem like we are praying to Mary as a god. We are not. Instead, we are praying to Mary, as we do to other saints, to ask her to pray to God for us. For these reasons, we venerate Mary. We do not worship her. Mary, as the mother of God and the mother of the Church, is treated with reverence and compassion.

When Mary agreed to be the mother of our Savior, she knew the glory and praise would go to her Son, but she agreed anyway. This enormous sacrifice deserves and commands our respect and admiration. We can look up to Mary and use her as an example of the perfect disciple: she was selfless, loving, kind, and generous. Her altruistic actions should be modeled by every Christian and every human being in the world.

Another reason we do not worship Mary is simply because she is not God. Mary was a human being. She was divinely inspired, but she was still a mortal being.

What Does Tradition **Tell Us About Mary?**

Ian Bozant
Notre Dame High School, Sherman Oaks, California

Tradition holds that Mary's mother and father were saints Anne and Joachim. Mary lived her life like many other people of her time and place—as a poor, Jewish woman in a land controlled by Rome. It was a difficult and uncertain life. One can imagine Mary's response to the Annunciation, where the archangel Gabriel announced to Mary that she was to bear the Son of God. This had to have been a frightening message for Mary. In her time, to have committed adultery before marriage was a grave sin punished by stoning.

She had extraordinary faith and courage when she accepted the archangel's message. She gave birth to Jesus and, reading between the Bible's lines and pages, nurtured him, sharing her faith and trust in the Lord. Throughout her life, she continued to show her faithfulness by accepting the Passion of her Son with humility and by continuing her dedication to the community of Jesus's disciples.

Mary is truly a remarkable figure in the Catholic faith. Personally, I hold a strong devotion to the Blessed Virgin because I find comfort in her humanity. She experienced the pain of losing her Son and the agony of being mocked and ridiculed by many. Yet through all this, she remained faithful and obedient to the Lord's will. She is a source of hope for me and for many that our lives can be handed over in complete devotion to the will of God.

What Does the Church Teach About Joseph, the Husband of the Blessed Virgin Mary?

Matthew Giordano

Saint Rose High School, Belmar, New Jersey

Because such a great amount of his life lies in speculation, Saint Joseph is one of the most mysterious figures of the Bible. The only credible sources of his life are the Gospels of Matthew and Luke.

It is widely accepted that Bethlehem, the city of David, was Joseph's birthplace. Yet, the Gospel opens with Joseph's settling in Nazareth just a few months before the Annunciation (Mary's being told by the angel Gabriel that she would bring forth the Messiah and name him Jesus). Saint Joseph was a *tekton*, which generally means "craftsman." Therefore his trade could have necessitated the move. Regardless, it is probably at Nazareth that Joseph married Mary. Whether this happened before or after the birth of Jesus is debatable, though it is modernly accepted that they were only engaged at the time of Jesus's birth.

One of the widely accepted truths regarding Joseph is the Incarnation story, in which the angel of the Lord appeared to Joseph, letting him know that God gave Mary her child, and that Joseph should not be afraid to marry her (see Matthew 1:18–25). So Joseph did as the Lord suggested. Although God is Jesus's true father, Joseph fulfilled that role in daily life. He loved Jesus and treated him as his own son. The last we see of Joseph is on the quest to find Jesus, who had left his family to preach in the Temple at age twelve (see Luke 2:4–52).

This is the end of Joseph's role in the Scriptures, and many experts agree that Joseph was probably dead by the time of Jesus's public ministry.

Just as most of his life is, the death of Saint Joseph is shrouded in mystery. He continues to be one of the greatest enigmas of the Bible.

Is It Okay to Admire **People Who Are** Not **Christian?**

Madeline Eckenrode
Lancaster Catholic High School, Lancaster, Pennsylvania

Whether they are mothers and fathers tucking their children into bed at night with a kiss, or doctors working in a dangerous country to save lives, people all over the world are spreading love. Whether seen or unseen, they perform acts of heroism every day, yet some of them aren't Christian. Is it okay to want to be like them even if they don't believe in Jesus?

This is a question theologians and ordinary people have struggled with for years. If people don't know about Christ or choose not to follow him but still try to be good, shouldn't they still be worthy of admiration? The answer, according to the Church, is yes. We believe that all goodness comes from God, and when we see God's goodness revealed through the actions of a person who is not Christian, we should recognize God's presence and try to imitate that same goodness in our lives.

There are many nonchristian people, both historical and living, that we can look up to. One is the Jewish survivor of the Holocaust and author of the book *Night,* Elie Wiesel. After living through torture, starvation, beatings, death marches, and the death of his family at the hands of the Nazis, Elie Wiesel was still able to recognize the goodness of humanity. Because of his tragic experiences, Wiesel has spent the rest of his life trying to encourage peace throughout the world and prevent atrocities like the Holocaust from happening again. He also urges other people to do the same. Another is Mahatma Gandhi, who, through peaceful protests, helped his country (India) escape the repression and cruelty of its British rulers and gain freedom.

Throughout the years, popes have told Catholics to both respect and admire other religions. Wherever we see goodness, we should admire it and strive in our own way and in accordance with Jesus's teaching, to follow those who practice it.

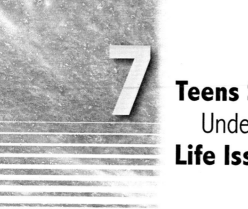

7 Teens Share Their Understanding **of Teenage** Life Issues

Does God Allow Bad Things **to Happen to** Good People?

Haley Watson
John Paul II High School, Hendersonville, Tennessee

Unfortunately life often confronts us with tragic situations that make us wonder about God's willingness or ability to help us. Why would a good God allow such things to happen? Doesn't God care? It is likely that everybody will ask themselves this question at some time in their lives. We all wonder why God allows illness, relationship breakdowns, failures of all types, and death to happen, especially to good people.

If there was ever someone who faced the issue of suffering, it was Jesus. (A close second is Job.) Jesus's life ended in pain, betrayal, and abandonment. As his life illustrates, something about the human experience says undeserved and bad things are going to happen to us. Yet this should not lead us to think God has left us. Neither the Scriptures nor Tradition give us an answer about why bad things happen to good people. But the Church does make it clear that good people do suffer and that their suffering is not a punishment sent by God.

Some mysteries, including suffering, can never be completely understood, only accepted. We cannot avoid suffering, but when we follow in the footsteps of Jesus, we can make it result in something good.

What Should I Do When I Disagree with What the Church Teaches?

Ian Bozant

Notre Dame High School, Sherman Oaks, California

It is likely that at some point in our lives, all of us will doubt and question our faith. Sometimes this can take the form of confusion or disagreement with Church teaching. Some of us get a "gut feeling" about the morality of a subject when we experience new issues and situations. This feeling leads us to either agree or disagree with it. Too often we stop there. We tell ourselves we disagree or agree with the Church based on immediate exposure to the issue.

As Catholics, and as the people of God, we are called to delve deeper into these topics to find the true meaning and the objective truth for ourselves. We are called to look into the facts and the foundations of the Church's teachings and the witness of the Scriptures. It is good practice to spend time in prayer opening ourselves up to the inspiration of the Holy Spirit. This will put us in a better position to examine the issue. Then, and only then, can we truly say we are ready to make a decision.

If we truly and sincerely form our conscience, we will find that the Church's teachings are objectively true. This may be frustrating to hear. We must remember that the Catholic Church has been around for a long time and has thought deeply on the concerns of daily life. We should have respect for, and openness to, this wisdom.

Is It Okay to Read Harry Potter Books?

Sean Barber

Saint Xavier High School, Cincinnati, Ohio

I read the first Harry Potter book, *Harry Potter and the Sorcerer's Stone*, when I was nine years old. I quickly developed an affinity for the boy wizard and his various coming-of-age misadventures, devouring the other novels in the series, my interest not waning but waxing over the years as I grew up along with Harry.

Harry Potter does not frighten me or cause me to question my faith; nor should it frighten or cause uneasiness for any other practicing, faithful Catholic (or Christian, for that matter). Harry Potter is not a series based on witchcraft and wizardry in the occultist sense (nor do I presume a hidden agenda on the part of the author). Rather, the books use magic as a literary device of imagination to draw the reader into a world inhabited by good and evil, right and wrong. The same can be said for J. R. R. Tolkien's (Lord of the Rings trilogy) and C. S. Lewis's (Chronicles of Narnia series) works.

The focus of the Harry Potter series should be on its ability to juxtapose moral values with the fantastic elements of the story. In a world where things are wildly spiraling out of control and evil forces are rallying around the antagonist (the symbol of evil for the series), Lord Voldemort, Harry Potter serves as a moral guidepost. He always acts with the best of intentions, even if his intentions do not always work out as planned. Harry values loyalty, friendship, and faith, and he puts himself behind the cause of universal good.

My Friend Just Told Me He Is Gay. How Should I Respond?

Ijeoma Okpara

Trenton Catholic Academy, Hamilton, New Jersey

Your friend has turned to you with a secret he or she has likely kept for some time. The good news, however, is that your friend has approached you because he or she truly trusts you and believes you are one of those rare friends who will stay by his or her side no matter what.

Most people who "come out" would like the same sincere acceptance and encouragement you might want when you tell a friend something special about yourself. You might first honestly ask yourself how you feel about this news and then discuss it as a caring friend. Some people who find out a close friend is gay wonder, "What does that mean for me?" This is a natural reaction. What it probably means is your friend trusts you. However, liking someone who is gay does not make you gay any more than liking someone who is smart makes you smart.

Homosexuals do not choose their sexual orientation. The Catholic Church affirms that people with a homosexual orientation are children of God and must be treated with compassion and sensitivity. As a result, we should stand up against any forms of prejudice and discrimination toward people who are gay.

I Just Started Dating Someone. How Far Is Too Far?

Kathryn Manocchia
Cathedral of the Immaculate Conception, Crookston, Minnesota

Dating for many is a way to discern who your future spouse is going to be. This can be a very exciting and enjoyable process if you keep the right perspective in mind, especially during your teenage years. Dating really should be seen as a temporary arrangement, a testing ground for relationships.

Some people will tell you sex is no big deal. Wrong! Sex is a huge deal. It ties two people together forever, even if they never speak to each other again. You can't escape the memories of sharing the most intimate act of all. That's why the Church wants us to save sex for the person we commit our lives to—the person we marry.

The Church also teaches that staying a virgin means more than just not having sex. It means keeping your mind, body, and spirit sexually pure. Messing around, touching each other in private places, and doing "everything but" just does not fit into that picture.

The Church teaches that sexual expression should be a sign of your commitment to another person. Real sex belongs within a real love relationship that will stand the test of time. The Church teaches that sex belongs only in the sacramental marriage.

When dating it is best to concentrate on getting to know one another emotionally and spiritually rather than going too far sexually. Remember that love comes first, marriage second, and sex third.

How Seriously Should I Take Someone Who Threatens Suicide?

Tommy Cheely
Northridge Preparatory, Niles, Illinois

Sometimes our own lives may not be perfect, and life can make demands on us that are not what we want. But the Church teaches that each life is precious to God. We can never throw a life away. The beginning and end of every life is up to God and only God. Suicide is the most sorrowful and destructive thing I've ever come across.

When you hear that someone you know is thinking about suicide, you might just try to ignore it, which is a common reaction. Or you might be scared to say anything about it because suicide is such a strange and difficult thing to talk about. But you have to overcome feelings of fear or disbelief, because if you don't do anything about it, you just might wake up one morning and find out that your friend isn't alive anymore.

Often people who are thinking of suicide really want to know that someone loves and cares for them. They are looking for someone to reach out and help them. If someone you know has threatened suicide, you should tell that person that she or he is not alone and that you want to help. Suicide involves mental illness and serious suffering, so don't think you can handle it all by yourself. You need to tell an adult, even if your friend tells you not to tell anyone else. Your friend needs professional assistance to help her or him get through this time of desperation.

The best way to support your friend is by encouraging him or her to seek out the professional and spiritual support he or she needs. You can help by sharing with your friend that God has a special plan for him or her, which not only involves him or her but also everyone he or she is meant to touch in life. Help your friend see that God values him or her, and so do the other people in his or her life.

Suicide causes devastation to the surviving family and friends, those closest to us. Pray for your friend and help her or him in every way you can. The effects of suicide are too grave to be ignored. Don't be afraid. Your friend needs your help.

My Older Brother Just Told Me He Doesn't Believe in God Anymore. How Should I Respond?

Morgan Watkins
Santa Fe Catholic High School, Lakeland, Florida

If your brother has told you he no longer believes in God, you should take him seriously and listen to his reasons for feeling this way. Don't overreact, and don't act as if his reasons are stupid or immoral. He will probably reply that he is still going to be the good guy he always has been; he just doesn't believe in God anymore. Listen to him openly, and then ask him what happened to lead to him to this point.

In an attempt to keep the conversation going, ask him to consider talking with you about life and faith for a half hour once a week. You can ask him any questions about his beliefs, and he can ask you any questions about yours. Use this time not to preach to him, but simply to ask him questions about life that could take root in his mind. For instance, if he believes that a God that doesn't answer him verbally isn't real, help him examine his thinking. Hopefully, as he considers the answers to these questions, he will slowly but surely see that everything in life points back to God, and he will eventually come back into a relationship with God.

Someone I Know Has Been Sexually Abused. How Can I Help Her?

Matt Lauber
Saint Xavier High School, Cincinnati, Ohio

If you've had a friend tell you she was sexually assaulted, you're probably feeling overwhelmed. It took a great deal of courage for her to acknowledge that she has been a victim of sexual abuse. In telling you, your friend has placed a lot of trust in you. Value that! Respect that! Protect that! And remember that she does not want your pity, but rather your presence and comfort. From my experience, I know that trust is the hardest thing to rebuild after a traumatic event. In some situations, your friend may need protection. Sexual abuse is illegal, so you and your friend must notify someone—parents, school authorities, the police—immediately.

Show your friend you love and care for her. Try to include her in everyday activities. Be there for her when she requests your presence, but also be sensitive to her need for time to herself. Understand that your friend may be hesitant to talk about the abuse. If that is the case, respect this request. Show your friend that she has value and that your life is better for knowing her.

Take the time to get in touch with your own feelings about what happened to your friend. The best solution I've found is journaling. I just wrote down my questions (and answers to those questions). My entry went something like: "Why did this happen?" "How do I respond?" "What does the future mean now?" "Do I need to change how I act?" "I wish I could help her with this." "How can I make her life easier?"

Finally, if you heard about the abuse from a third party (say a parent or another friend), don't broach the subject with your friend unless she initiates the conversation. Rather, be there for your friend, letting her know you care about her.

In Light of the Recent Sexual Abuse Crisis in the Catholic Church, How Can I Take the Church's Teaching on Sexual Morality Seriously?

Clare Albright
Saint Francis Central Coast Catholic High School, Watsonville, California

I remember when I first heard the sexual abuse reports. My response was one of disbelief. I couldn't believe that priests could do such things. I was sad, sick, and angry all at the same time. These feelings were made all the worse by the fact that Church officials tried to cover it up. It took me awhile, but I have been able to gain some insight and perspective to these tragic events. Clearly the illegal acts of some priests have caused serious injury to many people in the Church. Deep healing is needed.

Sexual abuse is sinful. However, the abuses committed by some Church leaders do not make the moral teachings of the Church less valid. Why should we stray from the truth of Church teachings given by our God just because others have faltered on the way to holiness? The teachings of our Church are inspired by the Holy Spirit, and they provide the way to wholeness, to full humanity, and to the Lord. Even when others fail to live up to the standards of our faith, we must continue to strive to live out the teachings of the Church simply because we believe those teachings make us more Christ like. We must recognize that all people falter, even those we look to for leadership in the Church. And we must remember that our faith is not in human beings; it is in our God.

What Does the Church Say About Violent Video Games?

Adam Jabs

Saint Xavier High School, Cincinnati, Ohio

Video games—the opiate of the youth, as some people call them. But the main point of this opiate is not to drive people toward disrespecting others or others' possessions. The main issue is how to control the game rather than letting the game control you.

I recall watching a special on television about the effects of these games. One person interviewed was a former soldier who compared the violence of games to the simulators used by the military. The difference is that people in the military are using the simulators to train for a job, not to be entertained. Video games are interactive movies where the hero accomplishes his goals in a way you choose. My point is that these games are left up to the imagination of the user, and it is the user's responsibility to game in a way that doesn't harm his or her moral values.

The Church has not yet directly addressed electronic games. As Christians, we have the right to enjoy leisure activities that help renew us.

Critical awareness and media-mindfulness skills are useful life strategies when applied to the games we choose to enjoy. Electronic games can be fun; they can bring people together to collaborate or can pit people against one another in competition. They can also be used excessively, unwisely, and uncritically. Being responsible and making good choices is key when it comes to video gaming.

I'm Trying Not to Have **Sex Before Marriage, but I Still Watch X-Rated Videos Every Now and Then. Is That** Okay?

Amy Morales
Saint Francis Central Catholic High School, Watsonville, California

Let me begin by congratulating you for trying to remain pure until marriage. But I don't think watching X-rated videos is going to help you in this commitment.

X-rated movies contain extreme violence and excessive sexual conduct. Our Catholic faith prohibits the watching of these types of videos for several reasons. First of all, the exposure to sex makes an idol of the human body and completely neglects that God was the one who made us. Simply put, pornography is dangerous because it violates human dignity. Pornography takes the gift of sexuality and makes it an object to be exploited and abused.

Even though people may agree to pose for these pictures or participate in sexually explicit videos, there is nothing right and everything wrong with viewing pornographic images. You also need to look at the risk of pornography becoming a sex addiction. Pornography can also lead to serious disrespect and even violence, especially toward women.

Don't get me wrong; sex is a beautiful thing—inside of marriage. Outside of marriage, it becomes recreational. Today society at large condones premarital sex. Our secular society preys on the degradation of women because "that's what sells." Our culture helps encourage people to believe that this type of lifestyle is okay, when in reality it is self-destructive.

There are better things to do with your time than watching X-rated videos.

What Should I Do When Friends Tease Me About Being "Too Religious"?

Jenny Morneault

Saint Louis Parish, Fort Kent, Maine

Many of us at times have been teased or hassled about our faith beliefs and practices. We are not alone. We need to tell our friends how this kind of teasing makes us feel. Most often when people tease us, they don't realize they might in fact be hurting our feelings. So we need to be honest with our friends about how their comments make us feel.

Even if we are the only ones in our circles of friends who are actually religious, and our friends make fun of and tease us for this, we should just think of how Jesus died on the cross to save us from sin. He didn't turn his back on us when we needed him. Why should we turn our backs on him?

For support—because at times we really do need it—we might consider joining our church's youth program or creating our own prayer or support group for friends who share the same beliefs as us. And most especially, we need to know that as young Catholics committed to our faith, we are not alone. Someday we may help someone become a believer. This might not involve anything we say, but might just be how we carry ourselves, the witness of our lives.

I Feel Distant from My Parents. How Can We Reconnect?

Candice Norrell

Saint Mary's University of Minnesota, Winona, Minnesota

It's always fun to reconnect with an old friend you haven't seen since grade school. You run into each other while shopping and the surprised "Ohmigosh! How are you?" follows. You talk about how life's been treating you, you exchange phone numbers, and you agree to have lunch sometime. You walk away from the conversation smiling and pondering how neat it was to run into that person.

So it is with your parents. Communication is key. Reconnecting with your parents is a hard task; take it from someone who's been there. Go to a football game with your dad and just talk about life! Tell him how school is, how work is going, and how you're thinking of trying out for the basketball team. Offer to go with your mom to the grocery store and chat with her about classes, your friends, and the new car you want. It isn't hard. Parents don't have to just be parents—they can be friends too.

One last point I'd like to make is that the fourth commandment is the first commandment that refers to something other than God. This commandment tells you how to love your neighbors, starting with those who are closest to you. That's pretty noteworthy. So pray for the ability to honor your parents. Praying for guidance from the Holy Family is also very important.

So put this book down, say a quick prayer, go find your parents, and ask them how their day is going. You won't regret it.

Is There Anything Wrong with Masturbation?

Anonymous High School Student

My addiction started back in grade school. This addiction is known as porn and masturbation. Back in grade school, my friends introduced me to something I had never seen before—porn. I thought seeing a naked woman in a magazine was the coolest thing. I knew what I was doing was wrong, but I didn't want to change. I made excuses to make it okay.

Then, at the same time, I knew if my mom caught me, she would be really mad at me. So whenever I would look at porn and masturbate, I would get so mad at myself for doing it. I didn't become truly aware of my addiction until last year when a teacher said, "You are addicted to something when you can't live without it." When he said this, I realized that every time I logged onto the Internet, I would be logging onto some porn site. The only time I wouldn't log onto a site like that was when my parents were home. This past summer, I took responsibility for my actions. I told myself that just because a lot of my friends view porn doesn't mean that I have to view porn. I also realized why I looked at so much porn. I was using porn to fulfill my sexual fantasies.

I can appreciate now why the Church is against pornography and masturbation. The human body is beautiful but becomes simply an object when we focus on specific parts. Likewise, the pleasure one receives from sex is meant to be enjoyed and expressed within the context of marriage, not done solely by oneself.

I've Started to Drink Heavily on Weekends. I'm Scared I Might Have a Problem. What Can I Do to Get Help?

Bobby Tonnies
Rockhurst High School, Kansas City, Missouri

If you find yourself with a drink in your hand, you are not alone. According to the National Center on Addiction and Substance Abuse at Columbia University, more than five million high schoolers binge drink at least once a month. Alcohol misuse and abuse among American teenagers has evolved into an epidemic.

Most of us know that the effects of alcohol abuse are long-ranging and can, in fact, be life destroying. So it is imperative that you begin to rethink the choices you are making and, if necessary, seek help from the people around you. Begin with your friends. Are they the ones inviting you to parties? Are they the ones applying the peer pressure? Surround yourself with people who won't promote this negative influence in your life.

Seek help in your family. Your family exists to take care of, support, and help you. Take refuge in this support.

If you find your misuse or abuse of alcohol cannot be avoided and defeated on your own terms, then seek professional help before your situation gets too out of hand.

Finally, remember that God understands the threat of alcohol and other abusive substances. God is ready to listen. God is always hoping you will turn to God and ask for help in changing your lifestyle.

My Girlfriend Is Pregnant. What Should I Do?

Kelly Coady
Bishop Watterson High School, Columbus, Ohio

This is a very difficult experience for anyone, but even more so for teenagers. Rather than be excited about welcoming a new life, you are likely experiencing confusion, frustration, and anger. Though you might be tempted by the "we can fix it" or "make it go away" attitude, you should know that the Church teaches that all human life is sacred and therefore abortion should *never be* an option. Abortion intentionally stops the development of an unborn child. Though abortion is legal in this country, remember that acts that are legal are not always moral. Abortion is a serious sin and is strongly forbidden by the Law of God.

Rejecting abortion does not mean you don't have choices. Raising the child or choosing adoption are both viable options for you and your girlfriend. The guiding principle in your decision-making process should be what is best for your child.

As difficult as it will be to tell others, it is in your best interest (and the developing child's) to seek advice from counselors and your families. When you are deciding whether to keep your child, you must think about how you will support your baby. Like any parent wishes for their children, you want your child to have a life full of opportunities. Sometimes this may mean the child will be better off with a family that can give him or her the love and support you are unable to offer at this time in your life. Often the responsibilities are too much for a teenager to bear. Know that adoption is a loving choice.

If you do decide to keep the child, remember that she or he is a great responsibility that will be with you for the rest of your life, even if you do not stay with your girlfriend. In the end, make sure your final decision has the child's best interest at heart.

Acknowledgments

The scriptural quotations contained herein are from the New Revised Standard Version of the Bible, Catholic Edition. Copyright © 1993 and 1989 by the Division of Christian Education of the National Council of the Churches of Christ in the United States of America. All rights reserved.

The quotations on pages 17 and 18 are from the *HarperCollins Encyclopedia of Catholicism,* edited by Richard McBrien (New York: HarperCollins Publishers, 1995), page 664. Copyright © 1995 by HarperCollins Publishers, Inc.

The quotation on pages 24–25 is adapted from the "Scientific Research and Man's Spiritual Heritage" address of Pope John Paul II to the Pontifical Academy of Sciences, October 3, 1981, as quoted from "The Creation Story of Genesis: Does it Contradict Evolution?" by Michael D. Guinan, in *Catholic Update,* June 1994.

The quotation from the Eucharistic prayer on page 60 is from the *Sacramentary,* English translation prepared by the International Commission on English in the Liturgy (ICEL) (New York: Catholic Book Publishing Company, 1985), page 545. The English translation of the *Eucharistic Prayers for Masses of Reconciliation* © 1975. Illustrations and arrangement copyright © 1974–1985 by Catholic Book Publishing Company, New York.

The quotations on pages 68, 71–72, and 93 are from the English translation of the *Catechism of the Catholic Church* for use in the United States of America, numbers 1407, 1514, and 1032, respectively. Copyright © 1994 by the United States Catholic Conference, Inc.—Libreria Editrice Vaticana. Used with permission.

The quotation on page 74 is from *The Rites of the Catholic Church*, volume one, number 25, by the ICEL (Collegeville, MN: The Liturgical Press, 1990), page 715. The English translation of the *Rite of Marriage* copyright © 1969 by the ICEL. Copyright © 1976, 1983, 1988, 1990 by Pueblo Publishing Company. Copyright © 1990 by the Order of Saint Benedict.

The statistic from the National Center on Addiction and Substance Abuse at Columbia University on page 116 is taken from the Students Against Destructive Decisions (SADD) Web site, *www.sadd.org/stats.htm*, accessed January 9, 2007.

To view copyright terms and conditions for Internet materials cited here, log on to the home pages for the referenced Web sites.

During this book's preparation, all citations, facts, figures, names, addresses, telephone numbers, Internet URLs, and other pieces of information cited within were verified for accuracy. The authors and Saint Mary's Press staff have made every attempt to reference current and valid sources, but we cannot guarantee the content of any source, and we are not responsible for any changes that may have occurred since our verification. If you find an error in, or have a question or concern about, any of the information or sources listed within, please contact Saint Mary's Press.

Endnotes Cited in Quotations from the *Catechism of the Catholic Church*

1. *Sacrosanctum concilium* 73; cf. Codex Iuris Canonici, cann. 1004 §1; 1005; 1007; Corpus Canonum Ecclesiarum Orientalium, can. 738.
2. St. John Chrysostom, *Hom. in 1 Cor.* 41, 5: Patrologia Graeca 61, 361; cf. *Job* 1:5.

"*Why Do Catholics* . . . ? addresses not only perennial questions about Catholic belief and practice (e.g., Why does the Catholic Church have a pope?), but also questions that are tangibly real to young people (e.g., How should I respond to my friend who just told me he is gay?) and questions that are contemporary (e.g., What is the controversy about *The Da Vinci Code?*). The answers from teens across the country express the Church's teachings in straightforward terms. This book is a valuable resource for teachers, youth ministers, and pastors who wish to communicate Church teaching in an accessible way to young people. The broad range of questions and the concise, honest answers will stimulate lively discussion."

—**William Madges,** professor of theology and dean of
the College of Arts and Sciences,
Saint Joseph's University, Philadelphia

Looking for More
In-depth Resources
for Exploring the Catholic Faith?

The Catholic Faith Handbook for Youth

With clear, concise information about the beliefs and practices of the Catholic Church—organized to parallel the *Catechism of the Catholic Church* so that young people can appreciate the richness of Catholic teaching—this handbook is the most comprehensive available. Teens will appreciate the articles and stories that shed light on issues important to them.

Available from Saint Mary's Press
702 Terrace Heights, Winona, MN 55987-1318
Phone: 800-533-8095
Fax: 800-344-9225
E-mail: *smpress@smp.org*
Web site: *www.smp.org*